CONFLICT
IRAQ

CONFLICT
IRAQ

WEAPONS AND TACTICS
OF THE US AND IRAQI FORCES

DAVID MILLER

MBI

This edition first published in 2003 by MBI Publishing Company,
Galtier Plaza, Suite 200, 380 Jackson Street, St. Paul, MN 55101-3885 USA

The information in this book is true and complete to the best of our knowledge. All
recommendations are made without any guarantee on the part of the author or publisher,
who also disclaim any liability incurred in connection with the use of this data
or specific details.

We recognize that some words, model names and designations, for example, mentioned
herein are the property of the trademark holder. We use them for identification
purposes only.

This is not an official publication

MBI Publishing Company books are also available at discounts in bulk quantity for
industrial or sales-promotional use. For details write to Special Sales Manager at
Motorbooks International Wholesalers & Distributors,
Galtier Plaza, Suite 200, 380 Jackson Street, St. Paul, MN 55101-3885 USA

Library of Congress Cataloging-in-Publication Data Available

ISBN 0-7603-1592-2

Credits
Project Manager: Ray Bonds
Designers: Hardlines Ltd, Charlbury, Oxford
Reproduction: Anorax Imaging Ltd
Printed and bound in the United States of America

The Author
David Miller is a former officer in the British armed forces. He spent his service in England,
the Falkland Islands, Germany, Malaysia, the Netherlands, Scotland, and Singapore. He
subsequently worked as a freelance author and for three years as a journalist for Jane's
Information Group, including as a staffer on the authoritative *International Defense Review*. He
was Editor of the two-volume *Jane's Major Warships,* and has written more than forty other
works, many of them related to modern weapons and warfare.

Acknowledgments
The publishers thank the various official institutions and other organizations and agencies
(including the United Nations, US Central Intelligence Agency, US Defense Intelligence
Agency, the Joint Intelligence Committee of the British Government, US Special
Operations Command, and individual armed services, and the US Defense Visual
Information Center), as well as private photograph agencies and individuals, for
providing information, references for illustrations, and photographs for this book.

Contents

THE LEAD-IN TO WAR

"Baghdad for now appears to be drawing a line short of conducting terrorist attacks with conventional or C.B.W. [chemical and biological weapons] against the United States. Should Saddam conclude that a US-led attack could no longer be deterred, he probably would become much less constrained in adopting terrorist actions. Such terrorism might involve conventional means, as with Iraq's unsuccessful attempt at a terrorist offensive in 1991, or C.B.W. Saddam might decide that the extreme step of assisting Islamist terrorists in conducting a W.M.D. [weapons of mass destruction] attack against the United States would be his last chance to exact vengeance by taking a large number of victims with him."

– from a CIA letter to the Senate, 7 October, 2002

In the Old Testament, Samson's final act was to use his great strength to drag down the temple, thus achieving not only its destruction, but also his own. Today, some observers are seriously concerned that Iraq's leader, Saddam Hussein, will do the same and that, as he crashes to defeat in a war against Iraq led by US forces, he will attempt to destroy as much as he can by whatever means are available to him – the "Samson option."

This book seeks to identify the problems and dilemmas facing both sides as they braced for war in 2003.

The traditional prelude to war is that troop movements increase, units go "on exercise" to areas of intended operations but then do not return as scheduled, and the flow of information to the public simply dries up. The situation in late 2002 met all those criteria and it became clear that

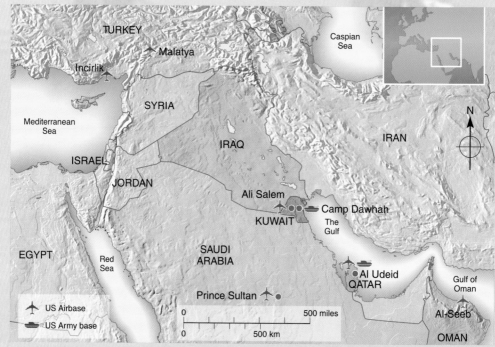

▲ **Above**   *Iraq is surrounded by unfriendly states. It fought a war with Iran 1981-88 and with Kuwait and Saudi Arabia in 1990-91. Jordan and Syria are hostile, and Turkey has served as a base for US/UK patrols.*

Below *US Army M1A2; king of the desert in 1991 and again in 2003.*

war with Iraq was imminent. But any attempt to assess the actual strengths and deployments immediately prior to the start of the war, particularly where the US and her allies are concerned, could be based only on scanty information which, in any case, would become rapidly out of date in the fluidity of the situation.

The Legacy of the 1991 Gulf War

The roots of the present situation stretch back many decades, but for the purposes of this book we need look no further than the conclusion of the 1991 Gulf War. Then, Iraq, having been totally and humiliatingly defeated, signed up to a series of UN National Security Council requirements. Among the most important of these were the unmasking, verification and then destruction of its apparatus for research and production of its weapons of mass destruction

(WMD). Beginning in April 1991, the UN Security Council passed a series of resolutions establishing the authority of the UN Special Commission (UNSCOM) and the International Atomic Energy Agency (IAEA) to carry out the work of dismantling Iraq's arsenal of chemical, biological and nuclear programs and Scud-type ballistic missiles. This resulted in the deployment of a large UN inspection team, which was hampered at every stage by the Iraqis and which withdrew after strong protests, its work unfinished, in 1998.

In a separate development, Saddam Hussein continued a program of internal repression against Iraqi Kurds in the north and the Shia Muslims in the marshlands in the south. Saddam and his family and followers started a postwar settlement of scores with the Kurds and the Shia, prompting the

establishment of two "no-fly" zones, which have continued in operation ever since, policed by aircraft of the United States and United Kingdom. These operations have curbed the worst excesses of Saddam against his fellow Iraqis, and have involved actual and "feint" attacks by Iraqi air defense forces against US and British aircraft, prompting many retaliatory strikes against a variety of Iraqi military targets.

This situation might have dragged on for several more years, but for the intervention of the terrrorist organization al-Qaeda (another spelling of which is "al-Qa'ida"), the evil attacks of 11 September 2001, and the resulting overt start of the US war against terrorism. For the US leadership, the invasion of Afghanistan in the hunt for al-Qaeda's leader, Usama bin Laden, was just the first stage in that war. The next step is the elimination of Saddam Hussein's evil and dangerous regime, which the US administration is convinced is linked to al-Qaeda. The following remarks were included in a CIA statement dated 7 October, 2002:

"Our understanding of the relationship between Iraq and al-Qa'ida is evolving and is based on sources of varying reliability. Some of the information we have received comes from detainees, including some of high rank.

▼ **Below** *UN inspectors take mustard agent samples from artillery projectiles wrapped in plastic to minimize contamination*

▲ **Above** *Following the 1991 war, UN weapons inspectors explode four rocket warheads that had previously carried Sarin nerve agent.*

UN/DPI Photos

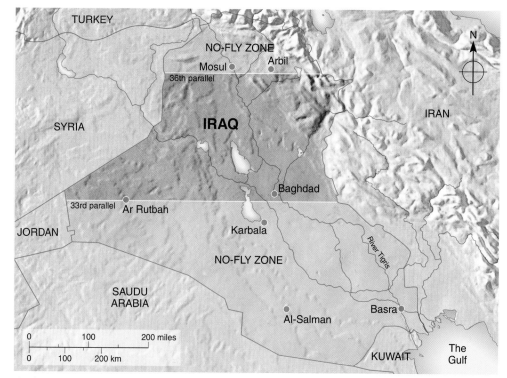

▲ **Above** *Iraq is about twice the size of the US state of Idaho and has land boundaries with six neighbors, but only very limited access to the sea. The North and South "No-Fly Zones" are policed by US and UK aircraft.*

We have solid reporting of senior level contacts between Iraq and al-Qa'ida going back a decade.

Credible information indicates that Iraq and al-Qa'ida have discussed safe haven and reciprocal nonaggression.

Since Operation Enduring Freedom, we have solid evidence of the presence in Iraq of al-Qa'ida members, including some that have been in Baghdad.

We have credible reporting that al-Qa'ida leaders sought contacts in Iraq who could help them acquire W.M.D. capabilities. The reporting also stated that Iraq has provided training to al-Qa'ida members in the areas of poisons and gases and making conventional bombs.

Iraq's increasing support to extremist Palestinians coupled with growing indications of a relationship

Right ▶ *US Army infantrymen are in place, ready for action following exercises simulating a desert war that could take place over the horizon.*

with al-Qa'ida, suggest that Baghdad's links to terrorists will increase...."

Poised to Strike

The United States has maintained a much higher presence in the area than before 1991 and, as a result, is much better balanced and poised to strike. EUCOM (US European Command) has been responsible for patrolling the northern "no-fly" zone (Operation Northern Watch), which has involved some 1,700 US Air Force and several

hundred British Royal Air Force (RAF) personnel, as well as fighter/attack, reconnaissance and tanker aircraft, plus US and UK special forces, based at Incirlik AB in Turkey.

The Gulf area is the responsibility of the Continental US (CONUS)-based CENTCOM (Central Command), which has maintained forces in the area ever since 1991. During the late 1990s the numbers of US military personnel, ships and aircraft in the area fluctuated on a daily basis, but

Country	Population	Army	Air Force	Navy	Others	Defense budget (US$)
Afghanistan	22,567,000	n.k	n.k.	0	0	n.k.
Bahrain	626,000	8,500	1,000	1,500	0	306m
Egypt	70,615,000	320,000	29,000	19,000	400,000	2.5bn
Iran	68,215,000	325,000	45,000	18,000	125,000	5.7bn
Israel	6,336,000	163,500	37,000	6,500	8,000	37.4bn
Jordan	6,900,000	84,700	15,000	540	10,000	520m
Kuwait	2,100,000	11,000	2,500	2,000	5,000	2.6bn
Lebanon	3,140,000	70,000	1,000	830	13,000	594m
Oman	2,674,000	25,000	4,100	4,200	11,000	2.4bn
Pakistan	161,838,000	550,000	45,000	25,000	288,000	2.6bn
Palestinian Autonomous Area	3,000,000	0	0	0	35,000	n.k.
Qatar	610,000	8,500	2,100	1,730	0	1.5bn
Saudi Arabia	22,205,000	75,000	20,000	15,500	106,000	27.2bn
Syria	16,493,000	215,000	40,000	6,000	168,000	838m
Turkemenistan	4,450,000	14,500	3,000	0	0	157m
Turkey	67,652,000	402,000	60,100	53,000	153,00	5.1bn
UAE	2,571,000	59,000	4,000	2,000	0	3.9bn
Uzbekistan	24,576,000	40,000	15,000	0	20,000	300m
Yemen	18,885,000	49,000	3,500	1,500	70,000	435m

Notes:
1. All figures are approximate and are based on IISS Military Balance 2000-2001 and CIA Year Book.
2. Figures for army, air force and navy are for active components only; reserves are NOT included.
3. "Others" includes air defense command (where this is separate from the air force), some types of police and interior ministry security police, gendarmerie, etc.
4. Defense budget is for 2000 or 2001 depending on available information.
5. No figures are possible for the Palestinian Autonomous Area.

Iraq's neighbors

was always approximately some 20–25,000 personnel, and about 200 aircraft and several dozen ships. This number then steadily increased from late 2001 onwards, and by late 2002 (and excluding forces deployed as part of Operation Enduring Freedom, the anti-terrorism campaign in Afghanistan) there were over 40,000 US military personnel in the Gulf area and 380 aircraft of all types. Some of these personnel were on lengthy assignments in the area – for example, in the naval HQ in Kuwait and the three Patriot batteries (one in Saudi Arabia, two in Kuwait) – while others were passing through on exercises, such as the Army series nicknamed Intrinsic Action and Desert Spring, which have routinely involved between some 2–5,000 troops spending two-three months in the region, primarily on desert training.

Naval units have included a headquarters and shore-based units of about 1,200 people, based at Manama in Bahrain, while another approximately 1,000 civilian mariners man the MSC (Military Sealift Command) ships based at Diego Garcia. There is always at least one Carrier Battle Group (CVG) in the area, plus another within easy reach, each of which has approximately 11,000 sailors embarked, plus some 90 fixed wing aircraft and helicopters, and, of particular significance, several hundred Tomahawk missiles in surface ships and submarines. There are also Marine Amphibious Groups, each comprising some 1,700

◀ **Left** *US Nimitz-class carrier refuels at sea during a long overseas deployment. The US has a decided advantage over Iraq in replenishment and resupply.*

▲ **Above** *USAF F-15s, capable of gaining air superiority and responsible for air defense of US land assets.*

▲ **Above** *Carriers and land-attack missile-armed destroyers – the cornerstone of US surface sea power.*

sailors, 1,500 Marines, and 700 Marine aviators.

Of particular importance to the US Navy (and to the forthcoming campaign) is Diego Garcia, part of the Chagos Archipelago. This is a British-owned island, located at 7 degrees South, off the tip of India and is shaped like a horseshoe some 15 miles long and enclosing a large lagoon. The island has an area of 6,720 acres, but is very low-lying, with an average elevation of four feet above sea level and the highest point a not very impressive 22 feet! The island is garrisoned by United States forces, and the facilities include a large airfield and living quarters, while the lagoon provides a natural harbor. The harbor provides moorings for pre-positioned strategic sealift ships, which hold equipment sets for two Army and one Marine brigade, as well as equipment to support Marine and Air Force aircraft. As of mid-2002, the airfield hosted the Air Force's B-52s of 40th Air Expeditionary Wing and the Navy's P-3 Orion maritime patrol and surveillance aircraft of Task Group 57.2, while preparations were being made for the arrival of B-2 stealth bombers.

Apart from using these "guest facilities," the Air Force operates air bases in Bahrain, Kuwait (Ali Al-Salem AB), Abu Dhabi (Al Dhafra AB) and Qatar (Al Udeid AB). The latter is also the headquarters for CENTCOM's Air Force Component, which commands all USAF assets in the region. Known Air Force deployments include 379th Air Expeditionary Wing (fighter/bomber aircraft, tankers and Joint STARS) at Al Udeid, 380th Air Expeditionary Wing (three recce squadrons) at Al Dhafra, and 386th Aerospace Expeditionary Group at Ali Al Salem.

A surprising development is the recent stationing of US forces in Djibouti, traditionally in the French sphere of influence, where there are now some 800 US troops, including Special Operations Forces, and an Air Force detachment that was responsible for the UAV which killed a wanted al-Qaeda leader in early November 2002. US Marines are also known to be undergoing desert training in the country.

Reinforcements are cloaked in secrecy, but it is already known that the US Army's HQ V Corps has deployed from Germany, that the Marines' HQ 24 MEU is on its way, and that the UK's HQ 1st Armoured Division has also been sent to join V Corps. There are also US forces and facilities in Saudi Arabia and Jordan, but but what will happen with these will probably not be decided until days, maybe even hours, before the attack begins.

Possible Battle Plans

It is scarcely surprising that the commander's battle plans have not been made public. However, it appears very probable that the assault on Iraq will start with a devastating aerial attack, by manned aircraft and cruise missiles. These will prepare the way for the ground attack by destroying the Iraqi air defenses and governmental facilities and will seek to paralyse the national infrastructure. The US has had eleven years to compile its data base of the location and status of Iraqi equipment, and the organization, dispositions and morale of its armed forces, so this aerial attack will undoubtedly be very effective.

One of the primary aims of this attack will be the elimination of the remnants of Iraq's Air Force, which will mean that there will then be virtually no air-to-air combat and the Iraqi commanders will be practically powerless to discover the deployment and intentions of the US and its allies. This will also be the first war to include what might be termed a "software campaign" in which the Iraqi computer and electronic systems will be either neutralized or destroyed by US computer systems.

This book concentrates on the major items of equipment and the major likely campaigns. Thus, the two main sections consider the land and air campaigns. While the US and

Allied naval forces will make fundamental contributions to both of these campaigns, there is no separate section on naval warfare as such, since Iraq is essentially land-locked and its naval forces consist of a small handful of elderly and badly maintained patrol boats.

Asymmetric Warfare

During 2002 there was political wheeling and dealing to line up a coalition against Iraq in 2003, along the lines of that formed in 1990–91. It is certainly true that Saddam heads up a vicious and thoroughly evil regime that has been guilty of a long series of brutal acts, many of them involving torture, mass murder and the use of chemical (definitely) and biological agents (possibly). However, the bottom line for almost all concerned is that Iraq is sitting on the second-largest oil reserves in the world, currently estimated at some 112.5 billion barrels. Only Saudi Arabia is richer in oil. Some of the opponents to a major military campaign – mainly China, France and Russia, together with a half a dozen other countries – have signed contracts with the present Iraqi regime to explore for petroleum or rebuild the country's oil infrastructure. Most of these contracts kick in once the UN economic sanctions are lifted. Such countries are fearful of the pronouncements by US State Department-sponsored Iraqi oppositionists, who have insisted that all such contracts will be abrogated as soon as the current regime is overthrown through a US invasion.

There is no doubt that the United States and its allies will outmatch Iraq's armed forces by a very considerable margin, and that while there may be near numerical

▲ **Above**   *The damage to the Pentagon, 11 September 2001. A total of 125 died in the building, another 64 passengers in the aircraft that crashed into what remains a high value target.*

parity in some cases, the qualitative margin is overwhelmingly in the US favor. In particular, the US will be able to detect virtually everything that happens inside Iraq, but the Iraqis will be unable to detect what the US is up to, and even if it could it would be able to do very little about it. What then can Saddam do?

In part he will continue to cause dissension between the US and other international actors such as China, France and Russia. Part of such a campaign will be the promise of major concessions once the threat of war has passed. He will also hope that a combination of innate patriotism in the face of what appears to be foreign aggression, reinforced by his thugs in the police, the Fedayeen Saddam and other security organizations, will prevent the general population from rebelling against him. He may also activate his own agents in the West who, in alliance with al-Qaeda, will carry out masses of terrorist attacks against very high value targets in the United States and Europe.

The "ace-in-the-sleeve," however, is Saddam's possession of chemical and biological agents. There is no doubt that at the meeting between US and Iraqi officials in Vienna in late 1990 prior to the Gulf War, a message was delivered to Saddam making it crystal clear what would happen to him and his country were he to use WMD in the coming conflict. In the event he did not, partly because he appears to have been assured of his survival and partly because of the threat, the contents of which have never been revealed, but which, logically, must have involved American use of nuclear weapons.

In 2003, however, there appears to be no chance whatsoever that Saddam will remain as president following strikes by US and allies. He may be permitted to go into exile to a country prepared to admit him, but the more likely possibility is that he, his family and his associates will die. Thus, if he is driven into a corner from which he can see no prospect of escape he may choose to use his WMD in what is known as "the Samson option" and drag the whole of the Middle East down with him in an apocalyptic final gesture.

> 66 **...he [Saddam] may choose to use his WMD...in an apocalyptic final gesture.** 99

WEAPONS OF MASS DESTRUCTION

"America must not ignore the threat gathering against us. Facing clear evidence of peril, we cannot wait for the final proof – the smoking gun – that could come in the form of a mushroom cloud."

–President George W. Bush, 7 October, 2002

The primary focus of a conflict with Iraq would be to disarm Saddam Hussein of his chemical and biological weapons, and also his capability of producing and using these and nuclear weapons in the future. The United States and her allies are convinced of the threat that Iraq's weapons of mass destruction (WMD) pose to the West and indeed to the world as a whole. However, while the United States has, as in all other aspects of its arsenal, formidable superiority in WMD, it is assumed that it would use them only as a last resort in the event of Iraq's use of such weapons against US and Allied troops and territory, or if the threat of such use was serious. Recent history suggests that the threat is serious indeed....

Under the leadership of President Saddam Hussein, Iraq has established a record of the development and use of weapons of mass destruction that is without parallel in modern times. What is even more chilling is that Saddam has not hesitated to use chemical weapons when the

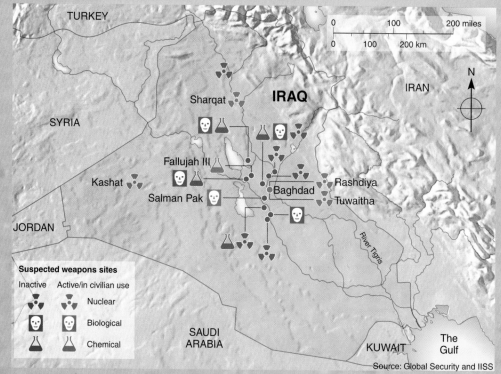

TURKEY

Sharqat

IRAQ

IRAN

SYRIA

Fallujah III

Kashat

Salman Pak

Baghdad

Rashdiya

Tuwaitha

JORDAN

River Tigris

Suspected weapons sites

Inactive   Active/in civilian use

Nuclear

Biological

Chemical

SAUDI ARABIA

KUWAIT

The Gulf

Source: Global Security and IISS

▲ **Above**   *The US assessment of current WMD-related sites operated by Iraq; establishing whether it is complete or correct was one of the major aims of the UN inspection teams sent to Iraq in late 2002.*

▲ **Above** *The Iraqi Kurd town of Halabjah is attacked by Saddam's forces in March 1988, using a deadly mixture of mustard gas, Sarin, Tabun and VX.*

▼ **Below** *Tents afforded Kurds no escape from Saddam's killers.*

circumstances seemed right and, while (so far as is known) he has not yet authorized the operational use of biological agents, his forces have certainly carried out trials.

The following is a brief description of the chemical and biological weapons known to have been possessed (some of them used) by Iraqi forces.

Chemical Agents

Mustard. One of the earliest chemical weapons, mustard gas is a burning agent, which was first used in World War One. Usually delivered in a shell or rocket warhead, it is a liquid, which gives off a vapor causing severe burns to exposed skin and eyes. If inhaled, it damages the respiratory tract and mucous membranes, and lungs. If ingested, it causes vomiting and diarrhea.

Tabun. Also known as "GA," Tabun was one of the earliest nerve agents; i.e., its primary effect is an unremitting attack upon the body's nervous system. It was developed in Germany as an insecticide and is a clear, colorless and tasteless liquid with a slightly fruity odor. The effects are very rapid, with chest tightness, vomiting, cramps, involuntary defecation, the collapse of the respiratory system and death. Death from a lethal dose in the respiratory system takes place within 1–10 minutes, and from skin absorption within 1–2 hours.

Sarin. Also known as "GB," Sarin is another nerve agent which originated in Germany, as a pesticide in 1938. It is a colorless, non-persistent liquid and the vapor is slightly heavier than air, so that it tends to hover close to the ground. Under wet and humid weather conditions, Sarin degrades swiftly, but its lethality endures with greater temperatures. Initial symptoms are headache and running nose, leading to vomiting and diarrhea, thence to convulsions and finally to death. Only minute quantities of Sarin are required, as was shown in the terrorist incident in Japan on 20 March 1995, when a highly lethal dose was released in the Tokyo subway system. This resulted in 12 deaths and 54 severe injuries. Approximately 1,000 people were affected to a lesser extent, but a further 4,000 sought medical help on the grounds that they thought that they might have been exposed; such fears were quite understandable, but added considerably to the load on the security and medical services.

VX. The third of Iraq's nerve agents, VX (V = venomous) was discovered by British scientists in the early 1950s while working on an insecticide, and then it was jointly developed with the United States as a chemical weapon. It is a persistent and highly toxic nerve agent, which, in its normal state, is a clear, odorless and tasteless liquid. Symptoms of exposure may occur within minutes or hours, and are generally similar to those for Sarin, but faster and more marked. In 1994 a Japanese terrorist group murdered an opponent by placing a tiny drop of VX on his skin.

Bacteriological Agents

Bacillus Anthrasis. This is a bacterium which causes anthrax infections through a cut in the skin (cutaneous), breathing (inhalation) or swallowing (ingestion). Virtually all cutaneous cases can be cured with proper treatment and even if no treatment is available about 80 percent of cases will usually result in recovery. The initial effects of inhaling anthrax bacillus resemble a common cold, but after several days the symptoms usually progress to severe breathing problems, nervous shock, and then death. Ingestion of contaminated food or liquids leads to intestinal anthrax, which is characterized by acute inflammation of the intestinal tract, with initial signs of nausea leading to loss of appetite, vomiting, fever, vomiting blood, and severe diarrhea; this form of the disease results in death in 25–60 percent of cases.

> **"Iraq has established a record of the development and use of weapons of mass destruction that is without parallel..."**

▲ **Above**   A UN inspector works patiently on an Iraqi chemical bomb.

▲ **Above**   UN inspectors wash each other down; the courage and fortitude of these people in the face of Iraqi WMD has been greatly under-rated.

▲ **Above**   Iraqi 155mm shell carries 3 liters of chemical/biological agent.

Aflatoxin. These are fungal toxins which act as highly potent carcinogen. They attack the liver, are capable of killing the sufferer years after ingestion, and also have particularly severe effects on pregnant women, frequently resulting in babies that are either stillborn or born with mutations.

Botulinum toxin. This is among the most toxic substances ever discovered. The initial symptoms may start to appear as little as one hour or as many as eight days after exposure. The effects lead to paralysis of the nervous system which results in death by suffocation.

Ricin. This is a very potent toxin, which is obtained from the beans of the castor plant (Ricinus communis), which are found around the world. The toxin is not difficult to produce, and Ricin is potentially widely available. It is used as a toxin in aerosol form and produces pathologic changes within 8 hours and severe respiratory symptoms followed by respiratory failure and death within 36–72 hours.

Delivery of Chemical and Biological Agents

The original means employed by the Iraqis to deliver their CW/BW agents was using 155mm artillery shells, which carry 3 liters of agent, and 122mm rockets, which have a payload of 8 liters. These shells and rockets can be delivered with great precision (for example, against a specific group of headquarters staff vehicles) but require a number of rounds to build up a sufficient concentration, and are, of course, limited in range.

Date	Agent	Target	Casualties (approximate)
Aug 1983	Mustard	Iranians/Kurds	<100
Oct-Nov 1983	Mustard	Iranians/Kurds	3,000
Feb-Mar 1984	Mustard	Iranians	2,500
Mar 1984	Tabun*	Iranians	<100
Mar 1985	Mustard /Tabun*	Iranians	3,000
Feb 1986	Mustard /Tabun*	Iranians	8–10,000
Dec 1986	Mustard	Iranians	Thousands
Apr 1987	Mustard /Tabun*	Iranians	5,000
Oct 1987	Mustard /nerve agents*	Iranians	3,000
Mar 1988	Mustard /nerve agents*	Iranians/Kurds	Hundreds

Authenticated occasions on which Iraqi forces have used chemical agents (nerve agents are marked *)

and poor standards of flying training, maintenance and serviceability. It would seem, therefore, that the only possibility of delivering CW/BW weapons by fixed-wing aircraft would be an occasional very high-speed, low-level mission, and even then only if the pilot was prepared to accept that he would be unable to return.

At least one trial has also taken place in which a Mil Mi-2 helicopter was fitted with a modified agricultural spray to deliver CW/BW as an aerosol. A helicopter flying low and slow would be effective only against totally unsuspecting and defenseless targets (e.g., civilians), and might not be very popular with the aircrew of the helicopter nor with the ground crew who would have to decontaminate it afterwards. The chances of such a helicopter penetrating US-controlled airspace seems very remote.

Next to be developed was a series of aircraft bombs, including at least four types with capacities ranging from 65–85 liters, considerably more than the artillery shells/rockets. However, this was still insufficient for the Iraqis, who went on to develop a weapon using an aircraft drop-tank, normally a means of carrying extra fuel, but which can now carry 2,200 liters of CW/BW agent. This very simple weapon has been tested with simulated CW/BW payloads.

Using manned aircraft to deliver these weapons presupposes that the aircraft will be able to penetrate enemy airspace. However, in any confrontation with the United States the Iraqis will find themselves in a position of considerable air inferiority even if all their aircraft were available and fully combat capable. As it is the Iraqi Air Force suffers from a combination of a shortage of aircraft

Delivery	Munition	Agent	Quantity (liters)	Date
Artillery	122mm rocket	Botulinum Toxin	8	Nov 89
	122mm rocket	Botulinum Toxin	8	Nov 89
	122mm rocket	Aflatoxin	8	Nov 89
	155mm shell	Ricin	3	Sep 89
Helicopter	aerosol spray	Bacillus Subtilis	8	Aug 88
Aircraft	bomb	Bacillus Subtilis	65	Mar 88
	bomb	Botulinum Toxin	65	Mar 88
	bomb	Bacillus Subtilis	85	Dec 89
	bomb	Botulinum Toxin	85	Nov 89
	bomb	Aflatoxin	85	Nov 89
	drop tank	Bacillus Subtilis/ Glycerine	2,200	Jan 91
	drop tank	Simulation – Water	2,200	Dec 90
	drop tank	Simulation – Water/Potassium Permanganate	2,200	Dec 90
	drop tank	Simulation – Water/Glycerine	2,200	Jan 91

Authenticated occasions on which Iraqi forces have tested biological weapons or simulated their use

The Iraqis are also known to have undertaken a development program to use surplus piloted aircraft as remotely controlled (i.e., pilotless) CW/BW delivery platforms. This program started with a converted MiG-21 fighter, which was tested in 1990, but after the Gulf War the trials have switched to the L-29 trainer aircraft. These aircraft have been fitted with an aerosol spray system, presumably related to that already tested on the Mil Mi-2 helicopter and MiG-21. It appears, however, that while the spraying system works, the remote control of the aircraft has proved a much more intransigent problem, and would be especially difficult in the face of the multitude of very sophisticated electronic warfare systems available to the USA.

The other means known to have been tested by the Iraqis is the use of CW/BW warheads aboard Scud-B and al-Hussein missiles. This was an ever-present threat during the 1991 Gulf War to both Coalition forces in the Gulf area and to the general population in Israel. In the event, the Scuds actually launched carried only conventional warheads.

▲ **Above**   *The sky above the Israeli city of Tel Aviv in 1991, as an incoming Iraqi Scud is attacked by a US-supplied Patriot missile.*

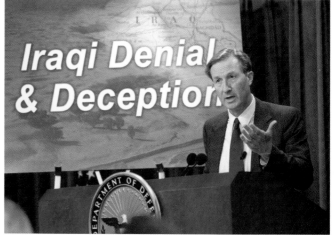

▲ **Above**   *Markings on the two nearest bombs show they were to be fitted with botulinum toxin warheads, something Saddam's men had denied.*

NUCLEAR WEAPONS

Iraq does not currently possess any nuclear weapons, but unless something is done to prevent it, there is a strong possibility that this can only be a decade away. Iraq started nuclear research in the 1950s and had made sufficient progress by the early 1980s as to pose a major threat to Israel, whose air force destroyed the reactor and research facilities at Osirak on 7 June 1981. The Iraqis then turned their attention to chemical and biological agents, but returned to their nuclear program during the Iran/Iraq War of the 1980s, when they set themselves the aim of developing a 20 kiloton (kT) nuclear weapon (i.e.,

▲ **Above**   *DIA briefer explains to reporters how Saddam hides his WMD programs from the rest of the world, 2 October 2002.*

a weapon of similar power to those used against Hiroshima and Nagasaki in 1945).

The Iraqi nuclear program was severely disrupted by the activities of UNSCOM after the 1991 Gulf War, when large quantities of nuclear-related material was located and destroyed. It became apparent in the mid- and late-1990s, however, that this had by no means put paid to Iraq's nuclear ambitions, and several attempts by Iraq to buy items such as aluminum tubing have been identified and stopped.

THE THREAT

Iraq has demonstrated a ruthless persistence over a period of some fifty years in its efforts to acquire weapons of mass destruction. Further, it has shown that attacks such as that on Osirak in 1981 and the UN embargoes and inspection programs of the 1990s have proved to be only temporary set-backs and have failed to persuade the Iraqi leadership to follow a more peaceful course. On every occasion the Iraqis have demonstrated an extraordinary resilience, and have managed to retain sufficient skilled people and research and production facilities to start over. In any war in 2003–4 there is no real danger of the use of nuclear weapons, but throughout any operations there will be a very real threat of the use of chemical and biological weapons, particularly if the Saddam regime is in extremis and, when faced by imminent and assured destruction, decides to take as many of the enemy with it as possible.

Such CW and BW might be delivered by missiles, aircraft or artillery (see map). However, there is also an unquantifiable threat that such weapons could be deployed against targets at a considerable distance from Iraq (for example, in western Europe or the USA) by individuals carrying small quantities of agent in a suitcase or backpack. The terrorist attack on the Tokyo subway clearly demonstrated the feasibility of such an operation and highlighted the vulnerability of sophisticated cities and their transportation systems.

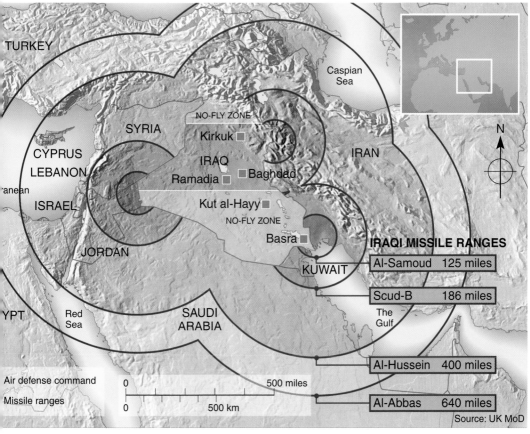

▲ **Above** *The range circles show the ever-increasing reach of Saddam's missiles. Nobody doubts that his primary target is Israel, but he would also aim at US force concentrations if he decided to use his deadly WMD*

THE BALANCE

The United States has an overwhelming advantage over the Iraqis in strategic weapons systems. It has many thousands of nuclear warheads mounted aboard more than 500 US-based Minuteman III and Peacekeeper intercontinental ballistic missiles (ICBMs) and over 400 Trident I/II submarine launched ballistic missiles (SLBMs), while strategic bombers (B-52, B-1B and B-2) can carry cruise missiles and gravity bombs armed with nuclear warheads. Suffice it to say that the US nuclear arsenal would be sufficient to flatten every city, industrial plant and military target in Iraq.

The United States is in the process of disposing of its chemical arsenal and it seems highly unlikely, for political reasons, that the president would authorize the use of biological agents in a "tit-for-tat" response. Thus, the only real counter to an Iraqi CW/BW attack would be either a completely unrestrained conventional air attack on a high-value Iraqi target, such as a city, or a single nuclear weapon, almost certainly against a military target, intended as a demonstration of the US administration's readiness to carry out a full-scale and devastating attack, if forced to do so.

◄ **Left** *Based in continental USA, Peacekeeper ICBMs, one of which is seen here with warheads being fitted, is one of the US president's strategic triad options.*

▼ **Left and below** *If Saddam uses his WMD, US retaliation may have to come from a nuclear arsenal that includes submarine-launched Trident missiles and B-1B bombers.*

IRAQI BALLISTIC MISSILES

Iraq's ballistic missiles (commonly and generically called "Scuds") may be relatively crude, slow, inaccurate and lacking in range and payload, but they pose a very real threat to US and Allied forces as well as to cities in neighboring regions. The payloads could be chemical or biological. Therefore it is vital that American forces (including Special Operations Forces, of which more later) track them down and destroy them at their launch sites or call in air strikes to deal with them. Failing that, the missiles must be destroyed before they hit their targets by Patriot anti-ballistic missile systems (ABM) or other air defense weapons.

In terms of a regional war the effect of Iraq's ballistic missiles is strategic. Between 17 January and 28 February 1991 the Iraqis launched 86 Scud missiles, all of the al-Hussein and al-Abbas sub-type (see below). Of those, five failed at or shortly after launch, and of the remaining 81, some 43 were aimed at targets, mainly US troops, in the Gulf and Saudi Arabia, and 38 against targets in Israel. The missiles were exceptionally inaccurate and at least 11 came down harmlessly in unpopulated areas, but seven did hit populated areas and caused US and Israeli casualties. Twenty-nine of the rounds heading for Saudi targets were intercepted by US Patriot systems, although debris from the incoming Scuds hit the target areas in about a quarter of these cases. Patriot systems based in Israel were less successful, even though the six batteries had the very latest software and were sent the PAC-2 missiles virtually straight off the production line.

▲ **Above** *Israeli troops and civil defense workers view the crater made by an Iraqi Scud missile during the 1991 war. In the event, Saddam did not use CW/BW, but nobody could know that until after the last missile had been fired.*

▼ **Below** *Iraqi Scud missile aboard its 8-wheeled launcher is caught in the open during the 1991 Gulf War. Such vehicles are mobile and difficult to find.*

When compared with US, Russian or Chinese strategic missiles, the Iraqi missile systems are very unsophisticated, lacking in range and payload, and extremely inaccurate. In the terms of a regional war, however, their effect is strategic, as was demonstrated in the Gulf War when Iraqi missiles landed on targets in Israel, Kuwait and Saudi Arabia. All Iraqi missiles are known to be inaccurate and to be capable of carrying relatively small warheads, but the problem is that the payload could well be either biological or chemical, and for those in the target area there is no telling whether this might be so until after the missile has landed.

With only one significant exception, all current Iraqi ballistic missiles are developed from the Soviet SS-1 Scud, which was exported to many countries in the 1960s and '70s. The first in the series, the Soviet Army's SS-1a was a mobile, tactical surface-to-surface missile system, first seen by Western observers in 1957. It was mounted on a JS-3 tracked chassis. But even the SS-1a was not an original design, having been developed by Soviet designers, helped by German technicians, from the World War Two German V-2 missile.

The Scud was carried horizontally on a transport-erector-launcher (TEL) vehicle, which raised it to the vertical and then placed it on a small launch platform, a process which took about 60–90 seconds. However, launch preliminaries in a new site took about an hour, which included site surveying, kinetheodolite tracking of upper-atmosphere balloons and fueling the missile, although this time could have been reduced if the site had been pre-surveyed.

All Scuds use an unsophisticated gyroscopic guidance system (again based on the V-2), which operates only during the powered flight phase, which lasts some 70–80 seconds, using movable vanes mounted in the motor efflux. The motor is shut down by a preset device which closes the fuel valves, and the missile then follows a ballistic trajectory to its destination. Unlike virtually all other tactical missile systems, the Scud's warhead does not separate from the missile body, but the entire structure continues, unguided, towards the target. This results in an inherently inaccurate missile, with the inaccuracy increasing with range.

In Soviet service, the Scud was developed thorough four versions, known in the West as SS-1a to SS-1d, the later versions having

Scud-B

Dimensions: Length; 36.8ft (11.2m); diameter 35in (89cm).
Launch weight: 13,900lb (6,300 kg).
Warhead: 2,200 lb (1,000kg).
Maximum range: 186 miles (300km).
Motor burn: approx 80 secs.
Accuracy: (cep) 1.2nm (1.4 statute miles/2.2km).*

In the early 1980s, Iraq acquired 819 Scud-Bs from the USSR for use in the war against Iran, - and many hundreds of these were launched against Iranian targets, although they proved to be very inaccurate and mainly of psychological and nuisance value. The Scud-B was some 1.63ft (0.5m) longer than Scud-A, the extra volume being used to increase the range. It was originally deployed on the same JS-3 tracked TEL as Scud-A, but was later deployed on the much more effective MAZ-543 8-wheeled TEL, with a revised and much more efficient gantry structure.

All of Iraq's Scud-Bs use kerosene as the fuel, combined with some form of oxidant, usually inhibited red fuming nitric acid (IRFNA). Following the 1991 Gulf War, Iraqi officials told inspectors of the United Nations Special Commission (UNSCOM) that Iraq had not experimented with UDMH (unsymmetrical dimethylhydrazine), a more powerful fuel than kerosene which is used in later Soviet Scuds. The Iraqis said that this would have required engine redesign for which they did not have the capability. Despite this assurance, the UN inspectors found evidence that Iraq had, indeed, carried out trials with UDMH, although it did not appear that it had been used in operational missiles during the Gulf War.

During and following the Iran-Iraq War, the great majority of surviving Iraqi Scud-Bs were modified in the al-Hussein program, although it is believe that five of the missiles launched in the 1991 Gulf War were original Scud-Bs.

*Circular error probable (cep) is the radius of a circle within which 50 percent of the missiles will land.

▼ **Below** *Iraqi Scuds are descended from the German V-2 of World War Two.*

al-Hussein

Left *Iraqi al-Hussein tactical missile, seen here on an Iraqi-developed trailer rig, is 37 feet long, and has 400 mile range.*

Below *Two al-Hussein missiles at an Iraqi arms show in the 1980s; their full significance was not recognized at that time.*

Dimensions: Length 41ft (12.5m); diameter 35in (89cm).
Launch weight: ca. 16,300lb (7,400kg).
Warhead: <1,100lb (500kg) HE/chemical.
Maximum range: 400 miles (650km).
Motor burn: ca. 80 secs
Accuracy: (cep) 1–2nm (1.14–2.28 statute miles/1.8–3.6km).

During the Iran-Iraq War, the Iraqis had a perceived operational requirement to be able to attack the enemy capital, Teheran, with missiles launched from bases behind Iraqi lines. The Iraqis adopted a very elementary approach, which simply involved cutting a missile in two and then inserting a 6ft (1.8m) "plug" cut from other Scud-Bs. They also halved the weight of the warhead. The resulting "stretched" version, designated the al-Hussein, carried some 11,000lb (5,000kg) of fuel and oxidiser, compared to 8,700lb (3,950kg) in the original Scud-B, and increased the maximum range to some 400 miles (650km).

However, these modifications were so crude and rudimentary that the missiles suffered from flight stability problems, particularly in the latter part of their flight envelope. This was partly due to alterations in the weight distribution and thus in the center of gravity, but also because the longer burn time increased the speed at cut-off, resulting in greater heating during reentry into the atmosphere than the original structure had been designed to take. These factors combined to make the missiles inherently unstable and on numerous occasions during the Iran-Iraq War and the 1991 Gulf War they were seen to break up when descending towards the target, although the warheads usually continued to the ground where they exploded.

Most of the 90-odd missiles launched against Bahrein, Israel and Saudi Arabia during the Gulf War were al-Hussein variants. At least 75 al-Hussein variants were filled with chemical or biological agents and were deployed but, so far as is known, were not used operationally. Following its defeat, Iraq was supposed to declare and destroy all its remaining al-Hussein missiles, but it is believed that at least 20 remained and more may have been fabricated from spare parts and components taken from other missiles.

al-Abbas

Dimensions: Length 47.6ft (14.5m); diameter 35in (89cm).
Warhead: 308–550lb (140–250kg).
Maximum Range: 500–560nm
(570–640 statute miles/920–1,024km).
Accuracy: (cep)1.9–3.1nm (2.2–3.5 statute miles/3.5–5.7km).

The al-Abbas program was the second attempt at a Scud modification, and the first prototype was flight-tested in April 1988. The airframe was 35in (0.89m) in diameter, the same as that of the Scud-B, but was a full 9.8ft (3.0m) longer. The additional fuel and oxidizer gave it a theoretical maximum range of 560 miles (900km), which put all of Iran, as well as the Gulf waters as far south as the Strait of Hormuz, within reach. According to one report, the al-Abbas was created, as with the al-Hussein, by cannibalizing propellant and oxidizer tanks from other Scuds, lengthening the size of the tanks, and increasing the amount of fuel. Additionally, the payload was reduced yet further, from 2,200lb (1,000kg) to a mere 308–550lb (140–250kg). As far as is known there was only one test flight in the period 1988–90 and the type never achieved production, let alone entered service. It can be assumed that it suffered from the same – and possibly worse – instability problems as the al-Hussein.

al-Samoud

Dimensions: Length 35.2ft (10.7m); diameter (missile)
21.6in (500mm).
Launch weight: ca. 5,070lb (2,300kg).
Warhead: Not known.
Maximum range: 93 miles (150km) (see notes).
(Data are for SA-2 Guideline – see text.)

The al-Samoud is the only Iraqi service missile not to have been developed from the Scud-B. Following the Gulf War, the Iraqis were placed under severe restraints by the United Nations and one method of trying to evade the strictures is this program to modify the SA-2 Guideline surface-to-air missile, of which the Iraqis possess large numbers, for a surface-to-surface role. The missile appears to be based fairly closely on the SA-2 but with modifications to the guidance and control systems, as well as to the engine, resulting in a range of between 60 and 90 miles, although both British and US intelligence estimates are that it is already capable of some 125 miles, if not more. The Iraqis originally gave this program the cover designation "J-1" but it has since been named al-Samoud (= steadfast). First flight took place in 1997 and since then a further 20 or so flights have been completed, all apparently successful. It seems highly probable that some operational missiles have been produced from SA-2s and are with field units.

increased range and being mounted on a more efficient TEL system. Various models of Scud were exported to Soviet "client states" in the Middle East and Asia, but only the Soviet Army version was ever nuclear-capable. Western observers, particularly the media, tend to use the term "Scud" as a generic description of all Iraqi missiles, but there were – and are – a number of major variants.

Another of Iraq's ballistic missile programs, the Badr 2000 missile project, while never reaching operational status, is nevertheless an interesting indication of Iraqi ambitions and problems. Missiles offer a nation such as Iraq the ability to strike at distant targets at considerably less expense, in terms of development, purchase and operation, than for an

air force equipped with conventional aircraft.

By the mid-1980s the limitations of the Soviet-supplied Scud missile were becoming obvious and it was clear that the basic design would not allow any further significant development. Iraq's two basic requirements were for greater range and increased payload and so, in the mid-1980s, a tripartite cooperative

▲ **Above** *After the 1991 war, UN arms inspectors prepare MAZ TELs for destruction. The vehicles and missiles posed a serious threat to the stability of the Coalition, out of all proportion to their numbers.*

program was established with Argentina and Egypt, for a 2-stage missile with a range of some 620 miles (1,000km).

The project was designated Badr 2000 by Egypt and Iraq, and Condor II by Argentina, with various versions being developed. The first stage was common to all and was solid-fueled, but the second stage was either solid-fueled (Egypt and Iraq) or liquid-fueled (Argentina). There were also reports that yet another version would have placed the Argentinean liquid-fueled second stage atop the solid-fueled first and second stages to give a 3-stage missile capable of undertaking space missions. Basic specifications (for the Egypt/Iraq 2-stage missile) were: length 33.8ft (10.3m); diameter 31.5in (0.8m); launch weight 10,582lb (4,800

kg); warhead: HE – 772lb (350kg); maximum range ca. 621 miles (ca. 1,000 km); accuracy not known.

The project was cloaked in secrecy and was under the general direction of the Arab League Industrial Development Organisation, whose headquarters were located in Baghdad. In general terms, Iraq was responsible for finance, Argentina for development of the missile and design of the production facilities (which would be located in Iraq), and Egypt for coordinating the technology, which involved a large number of US and European firms.

Progress was slow, due to a combination of factors, mainly the need for secrecy, the lack of missile technology and expertise among the three partners, a certain amount of mutual suspicion and intense

opposition from the international community. Frustrated by the lack of progress, Iraq gradually assumed a greater role and established three sites for use in the development program, which they now gave the cover name of "Project 395". As far as is known, however, no missiles were ever produced and all facilities and equipment declared by Iraq to the UN Commission following the Gulf War were destroyed.

It is believed that, prior to its demise, Project 395 had achieved reasonable progress in the design of the missile and development of the solid-fuel engine, but rather less in the matters of guidance and control. It can also be assumed that technological lessons learnt by Iraq during the Badr 2000 program have been applied to other national missile projects.

▲ **Above** *US SOF in the desert on a "Scud-hunting" operation during the 1991 Gulf War. Such activities were essential to keep the Israelis out of the war, which would have led to some (maybe all) Arab forces quitting the Coalition.*

Launch Sites

The great majority of Iraqi ballistic missiles are carried by the highly effective if somewhat elderly Soviet-made MAZ-543 8-wheeled transporter-erector-launcher (TEL), although some other, more modern vehicles are believed to have been modified for the task. A battery will normally comprise one or two launchers, a vehicle towing a spare missile, a command vehicle and a fueling vehicle.

Counter-action

As was demonstrated during the 1991 Gulf War, there are only two methods of countering the threat posed by Scud-type missiles. One is to hunt down and destroy the launchers before the missile can be fired; the other is to destroy the incoming missile using an interceptor missile such as the Patriot. The US Army's Patriot demonstrated an ability to destroy Scuds in the Gulf War, although subsequent analysis showed that fewer hits were scored than had been claimed at the time. However, there have been many upgrades to the Patriot in the intervening twelve years, while there has been none of any consequence to the Iraqi missiles.

MIM-104 Patriot (PAC-2)

Manufacturer: Raytheon, USA.

Type: Single-stage, low-to-high-altitude air defense missile system.

Weight: 1,984lb (900kg).

Dimensions: length 17.0ft (5.2m); diameter 16in (41cm); finspan 36.2in (92cm).

Propulsion: Single-stage solid propellant rocket motor.

Performance: Max speed Mach 5; range 43.5–99 miles (70–160km); minimum range 1.9 miles (3 km); max altitude 75,500ft (23km); time of flight 9–210 seconds.

Warhead: HE blast with proximity fuze; 200lb (91kg).

Guidance: Command guidance with TVM and semi-active homing.

Platform: Four-round mobile trainable semi-trailer.

(Data for Patriot PAC-2 missile.)

▲ **Above** *The Patriot's multi-function radar.*

◀ **Left** *Patriot missile leaves its launcher.*

Patriot was developed as a successor to Nike-Hercules and the US Army's Hawk. It had a lengthy gestation period; the operational requirement was finalised in 1961, but development was not completed until 1982. The main reason for the delay was the complexity of the system, particularly of the track-via-missile (TVM) radar guidance, but since the problems have been overcome Patriot has proved a success. Conceived for use against aircraft, it was later decided to add an anti-tactical ballistic missile (TBM) capability, resulting in the Patriot Advanced Capability-One (PAC-1) system, first flown in 1986, which included software enhancements to enable the phased array radar to view angles from 45deg up to nearly 90deg.

This was quickly followed by PAC-2, in which the missile had an improved warhead and fuze, while the radar was again enhanced, this time to enable it to detect smaller targets. PAC-2 began flight tests in 1987 and was in service in time to be deployed in Operation Desert Storm in 1991, where it showed an ability to destroy Scuds; subsequent analysis proved that it had not been as successful as had been thought, but there is no doubt that its very presence considerably boosted morale.

PAC-2 Configuration 1 was deployed in 1993 and included the Guidance Enhancement Missile – PAC-2(GEM) – and improvements in the system's battle management, command, control, communications and intelligence (BMC3I), all primarily intended to accelerate the handling process and expedite missile launch. PAC-2 Configuration 2 was fielded in 1998, involving yet further improvements to the radar, communications, and other systems. Work is now in hand on PAC-3 which involves a new, smaller interceptor which, in conjunction with an enhanced radar and other improvements, results in a major advance in the system as a whole.

A Patriot firing battery includes the radar set, engagement control station (ECS) and up to 16 launching stations, which are supported by the usual sections providing power, communications, maintenance and administration. During air defense operations the ECS is the operations control center of the battery and is the only element to be manned. The ECS contains the weapons control computer (WCC), man/machine interface and various data and communication terminals. The M901 Launching Station transports, points and launches four missiles and is entirely remotely operated, via either a VHF radio or fiberoptic data link from the ECS. The launchers can be up to 0.6 miles 1,100yd from the ECS. The MPQ-53 phased-array radar has a range of up to 62 miles, can track up to 100 targets and can provide missile guidance data for up to nine missiles.

The Patriot missile is equipped with a track-via-missile (TVM) guidance system. Mid-course correction commands are transmitted to the guidance system from the ECC. The target acquisition system in the missile acquires the target in the terminal phase of flight and transmits the data using the TVM downlink via the ground radar to the ECC for final course correction calculations, which are then transmitted to the missile. The high explosive 198lb warhead is situated behind the terminal guidance section.

Patriot will be in the front-line in a 2003 war against Iraq, who will undoubtedly launch ballistic missiles against US and allied targets. There has been twelve years' development since the Gulf War and there can be no doubt that the latest Patriot system is considerably improved; it will give a good account of itself in defending against Iraqi missiles.

THE AIR CAMPAIGN

Despite the fact that Iraq suffered a humiliating and devastating defeat of its Air Force and air defense assets in 1991, Saddam Hussein, who has scant regard for the sufferings of his people, seems determined to expose them to yet more attacks by the mightiest concentration of air power the world has ever known.

From Saddam down to the man in the downtown Baghdad coffee shop, or to the shepherd with his flock in the Iraqi marshes, there can have been nobody in the country who was not aware of the air power demonstrated by the United States in the 1991 Gulf War. Mighty B-52 bombers inflicted damage from great heights and with pinpoint accuracy while cruise missiles launched from surface warships and submarines literally followed the street map as they worked their way relentlessly towards their targets. Those attacks inflicted terrible damage. Nobody, anywhere in the world, had any doubts about the determination, resolution and power available to US commanders.

▲ **Above**   *The first attacks on Iraq will come from sea-launched Tomahawks.*

The United States' air forces are composed of strategic bombers, fighters and fixed-wing attack aircraft, all of which have repeatedly shown can be combined into a versatile striking force, capable of rapid deployment to any part of the world. They are designed to gain and then sustain air supremacy over their opponents in order to minimize friendly casualties and to open the way for attacks by ground forces.

Thus, the war against Iraq, as with the 1991 Gulf War – and also the attacks on al-Qaeda terrorists and their Taliban hosts in Afghanistan following "9/11" – will start with a massive aerial onslaught in which the full might of the United States' air forces will devastate Saddam's meager and dispirited resources. One of the US commanders' aims will be to eliminate what remains of the Iraqi Air Force as quickly as possible, using a combination of bombs against the enemy aircraft, runways and shelters, and conventional air fighting tactics. Against the very best equipment available, the Iraqis will be unable to resist.

One of the features that will rapidly become apparent, as it did in the Gulf War, is that a significant number of American aircraft types can operate around the clock. The pilots' radars, terrain avoidance sensors and night vision goggles (NVG) insure that the Iraqi leadership comes under unremitting pressure 24 hours a day, seven days a week, with darkness and bad weather not offering any respite.

Most of the aircraft will operate from airbases within the theater, including those in Bahrein, Kuwait and Oman. Others will come from carriers of the US Navy in the Gulf,

◀ **Left**   *The effect of the B-52's incredible ordnance-delivery capability was witnessed recently in Afghanistan.*

quantity and quality, those of Iraq. Apart from the continental US (CONUS)-based bomber forces, the current global total is 20 Air Force fighter wing-equivalents (FWEs) with 72 aircraft each; 11 Navy carrier air wings, operating 46 fighter/attack aircraft apiece; and four Marine air wings, which are task organized and include varying numbers and types of aircraft. In addition, the US Army currently operates some 1,340 armed helicopters, which are discussed under "The Land Campaign."

▲ **Above** *Everything in the design and equipping of the F-117 stealth attack aircraft is intended to deceive the enemy, and, as in 1991, they will join the first attacks on Saddam's evil empire.*

▼ **Below** *Launch of a 24-hour AGM-130 adverse weather stand-off missile from an F-15E.*

some from the remote island of Diego Garcia in the Indian Ocean, others from even further afield, their range extended by aerial refueling. Of course, the United States will face many problems – some of them political, as a few neighboring countries refuse to make airfields available or decline requests by US military aircraft to overfly their territory. But nobody can doubt that the aircraft will get through.

UNITED STATES AIR FORCES

United States aviation assets are huge and far outmatch, both in

Type	US Navy	USMC	US Army	USAF	TOTALS
Bombers	0	0	0	204	204
Fighters	936	360	0	2,207	3,503
Ground Attack	0	0	0	270	270
Recce	0	0	0	61	61
ASW	373	0	0	0	373
Transport inc Tankers	109	101	219	1,668	2,096
Electronic	192	20	51	31	294
C3	0	0	0	40	40
Obsn/FAC	0	0	0	118	118
Weather	0	0	0	21	21
Misc	0	0	0	5	5
Training	747	18	2	1,258	2,025
TOTALS	2,356	499	272	5,883	9,010

Notes:
1. Figures taken from IISS Military Balance 2001-2002.
2. Figures are for front-line airframes only and do not include those in store, deep maintenance, etc.

Fixed-wing aircraft of the US armed forces

Type	Navy	Marine Corps	Army	Air Force	TOTALS
Attack	6	188	1148	0	1,342
ASW	242	0	0	0	242
Utility	152	124	2,144	169	2,589
Heavy Tpt	91	438	452	38	1,019
Observation	0	0	772	0	772
EW	0	0	64	0	64
Training	130	0	135	6	271
TOTALS	621	750	4,715	213	6,299

▲ **Above** *US Army AH-64 Apache attack helicopter armed with free-flight rockets and Hellfire missiles.*

Notes:
1. Figures taken from IISS Military Balance 2001-2002.
2. Figures are for front-line airframes only and do not include those in store, deep maintenance, etc.

Helicopters of the US armed forces

Type	In service	Storage/support	TOTALS
HC-130 Hercules	22	5	27
HU-25 Falcon	20	21	41
HH-60J Jayhawk	35	7	42
HH-65A Dolphin	80	14	94
TOTALS	157	47	204

Aircraft of the US Coast Guard

Segment	Sub-segment	Main aircraft types	Strength
Long range	Passenger	A-301, B-747, B-757, B-767, DC-10, L-1011, MD-11	271
	Cargo	B-747, DC-8, DC-10, L-1011, MD-11	230
Short range	Passenger	A-300, B-727, B-737, MD-80/83	81
	Cargo	L-100, B-727, DC-9	14
Domestic/ aeromed		B-767	34
TOTAL			630

Aircraft of the US Civil Reserve Air Fleet

It is impossible to say which aircraft will be sent to the Gulf. The accompanying tables show the total strength of the US air forces, from which commanders will be able to select what they need for each phase of the campaign. It should be noted that these tables include the Coast Guard, whose assets come under the DoD in war, and the Civil Reserve Air Fleet (CRAF) which plays a vital role in deploying troops and equipment to and from operational theaters.

Media and public attention tends to concentrate upon the bombers, fighters and attack aircraft, which are at the cutting edge of airpower, and which deliver the direct blows upon the enemy. However, other elements play equally essential roles, but usually fail to gain the limelight. The Airborne Warning and Command System (AWACS) provides command and control (C2) over the battlefield, ensuring rapid and effective coordination of air assets, while the airborne tankers serve as force multipliers, enabling combat aircraft to achieve greater ranges or remain on station far longer than would otherwise be possible. Then there is the huge air transport fleet, consisting of strategic C-5s, C-17s and C-141s, the tactical C-130s, and battlefield

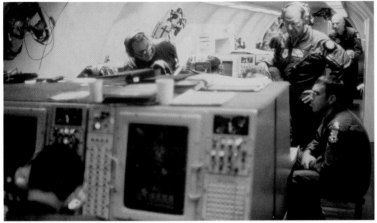

◄ **Left**   *Operators and analysts inside a USAF E-3 AWACS, one of the first assets to be deployed in any crisis. The aircraft's sensors enable operators to perform surveillance, identification, weapons control, battle management, and communications functions in real time.*

▼ **Below**   *The USAF's airborne tankers, such as this KC-135 refueling a B-1B bomber, are true force multipliers.*

transport helicopters that provide the means to move troops and equipment according to the needs of the operational commanders.

Most US aircraft will be based ashore, but there will also be a sizeable element afloat. The accompanying table shows the make-up of a US Navy carrier-based air wing.

IRAQI AIR FORCE

Facing this mighty air armada are the remnants of what was once one of the best air forces in the Middle East. Any assessment of today's Iraqi Air Force must start with the disgraceful events of a decade ago. By 1990 Iraq's Air Force had had much money lavished on it: the men were well-paid and equipped with some excellent French and Russian aircraft. These were dispersed at a number of major airfields, where most were housed in hardened aircraft shelters (HAS), which had been constructed under the supervision of Western engineers to the very latest Cold War designs and standards. In addition, each operational airfield had good ground-based defenses, with a mix of anti-aircraft guns and surface-to-air missiles, deployed according to the then Soviet practice.

Aircraft		Squadrons		Totals
Role	Type	Number	Aircraft	Aircraft
Strike	McDonnell Douglas F/A-18 Hornet/Super Hornet	3	12	36
Fighter	Grumman F-14 Tomcat	1	10	10
ASW	S-3B	1	8	8
	Sikorsky SH-60 Seahawk	1	6	6
Electronic Warfare	Grumman EA-6B Prowler	1	4	4
Airborne Early Warning	Grumman E-2C Hawkeye	1	4	4
Logistic Support	Grumman C-2 Greyhound	-	-	1
TOTAL				69

US Navy carrier air wing

▼ **Below** *F-14 Tomcat swing-wing fighters aboard a US Navy aircraft carrier. Responsible for fleet air defense, these powerful and well-armed aircraft are unlikely to find many targets due to the poor state of Saddam's air force.*

▲ **Above** *Northrop Grumman EA-6B Prowler is one of the best and most capable all-round ECM aircraft in the world, housing a multiplicity of systems to thwart the enemy by determining and jamming his electronic systems.*

▼ **Below** *F/A-18 Hornet of squadron VFA-131 Wildcats, assigned to carrier USS Eisenhower. F/A-18E Super Hornets, now joining the fleet in ever-increasing numbers, first deployed to the Gulf in late-2002.*

Despite all this, at the start of the 1991 Gulf War Coalition air forces inflicted devastating damage on both the runways and the shelters. Within a matter of days Saddam Hussein was faced with the dilemma that if his aircraft took off to fight they would be greatly outnumbered and quickly eliminated, while if they remained on the ground they would soon be destroyed anyway. The only solution left to him was to deploy them to a neutral country. Getting wind of this, Coalition commanders anticipated that he would send them to Jordan.

In fact in one of the most extraordinary events involving any air force since military aviation began, some 150 aircraft went to Iran, a country with which Iraq had only just ended a long and very costly war. The combat aircraft involved are shown in the accompanying table.

Aircraft	NATO Name	Role	Source	Number Fled
Sukhoi Su-20/-22	Fitter	Ground attack fighter	USSR	44
Sukhoi Su-24	Fencer	All-weather attack/recce	USSR	24
MiG-23	Flogger	Multi-role fighter	USSR	12
MiG-25	Foxbat	High-altitude interceptor	USSR	7
MiG-29	Fulcrum	Interceptor	USSR	4
Ilyushin Il-76	Candid	Military transport	USSR	15
Ilyushin Il-976	Adnan I	Airborne early warning	USSR/Iraq	2
Mirage F1	-	Interceptor	France	24
TOTAL				132*

* In addition, a number of civilian airliners also went to Iran.

Iraqi combat aircraft that "escaped" to Iran, January-February 1991

All these aircraft certainly survived, but the Iranians refused to return them and they languish on their airfields to this day. A few may have been taken over to be operated by Iran, but the others have simply fallen into disrepair.

Against this background, today's Iraqi Air Force consists of some 316 combat aircraft, of which the great majority were supplied by the Soviet Union or China, but a number of French Mirage F1s also survive.

In 2003 the Iraqi Air Force was something of an unknown quantity. Whether Saddam would again send his Air Force to another country, order it to fight to the last, or simply allow it to be destroyed piecemeal, will be seen only when the war starts. However, one scenario which must give concern to United States commanders is that, if Saddam thought that all was lost and that his personal survival was no longer even a remote possibility, then he might use a few of his aircraft, crewed by fanatics, to mount suicide missions against foreign targets, either among US forces or targets in Israel.

CRUISE MISSILES

The US attack on Iraq will start with cruise missiles, which have proved exceptionally effective in the past and will undoubtedly do so again. These are launched from B-52H (AGM-86) and from submarines and ship (Tomahawk). The Iraqis have no means of countering them and have no similar weapons of their own with which to threaten US forces. It might be possible to consider the UAV version of the L-29 turbojet trainer aircraft as a form of cruise missile, but it is large and its primitive guidance system will prevent it from seeking shelter by "nap-of-the-earth" flight profiles.

▲ **Above**   *The Su-22 has proved a durable, effective ground-attack fighter, but no fewer than 44 of Iraq's escaped to Iran in 1991.*

▲ **Above**   *Very few of Iraq's Mirage F1 fighters remain in service today.*

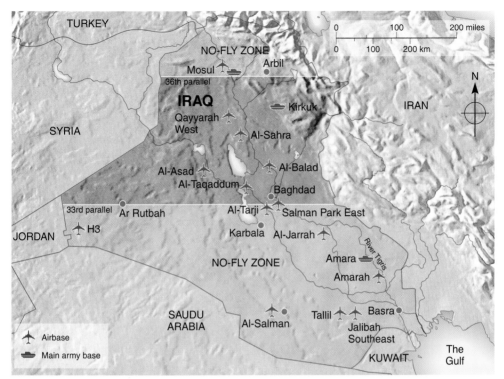

▲ **Above** *The location of Saddam's air bases is easy to establish by satellite imagery; what is much harder to assess is how effective the aircraft might be after 12 years of poor maintenance and shortage of spares.*

▲ **Above** *Four Chinese-built H-6s were supplied to Iraq in the mid-1980s. They were the same as the Chinese Navy version seen here, intended for maritime strike and armed with two anti-ship missiles.*

Role	Est total	Aircraft	NATO name	Source	Number	Remarks
Bomber	6	H-6D	Badger	China	2	Chinese version of Tu-16
		Tu-22	Blinder	USSR	4	
Fighter-Ground Attack	130	Mig-23	Flogger	USSR	20	
		Su-20/-22	Fitter-C/G	USSR	15	
		Su-25K	Frogfoot	USSR	10	
Attack	?	Su-24	Fencer-D	USSR	<3	
Fighter	180	F-7B	Fishbed	China	20	Chinese MiG-21
		MiG-21	Fishbed	USSR		
		MiG-25	Foxbat	USSR	<3	
		Mirage F1	-	France	15	110 ordered; 93 delivered
		MiG-29	Fulcrum	USSR	<3	
Tanker	?	Il-76		USSR	<3	Candid A/-B

Notes:
1. All figures are estimates.
2. Serviceability of fixed-wing aircraft is about 50 percent.
3. Flying hours: senior pilots 100-110, junior pilots less than 30.
4. All helicopters are operated by the Army.
5. No firm numbers are put on individual types due to the very high degree of uncertainty.

Iraqi Air Force combat aircraft, January 2003

AGM-86C/D

Manufacturer: Boeing, USA.

Type: Air-to-ground strategic cruise missile.

Weight: 3,150lb (1,429kg).

Dimensions: Length 20.8ft (6.3m); diameter 24.5in (62.2cm); height 4ft (1.2m); wingspan 12.0ft (3.7m).

Powerplant: Williams Research Corp. F-107-WR-10 turbofan engine; 600lb (272kg) static thrust.

Performance: peed approx 500kt (576mph/927km/h); range >600nm (690 miles/1,112km).

Guidance: Litton INS element integrated with multi-channel onboard GPS.

Warhead: Conventional blast/frag warhead; Block 0 ca 2,000lb; Block I ca 3,000lb.

Platform: B-52H. (Data are for AGM-86C.)

▲ **Above** *AGM-86 CALCM is launched from manned bombers.*

The AGM-86 Conventional Air-Launched Cruise Missile (CALCM) is among the most effective weapons of its type in the US arsenal. The nuclear-armed AGM-86B became operational in 1982. It is launched only from B-52H bombers, which carry six missiles on each of two externally mounted pylons and eight internally on a rotary launcher, giving a maximum capacity of 20 missiles per aircraft. Immediately following release, the wings unfold, tail surfaces and engine inlet deploy, and the engine starts. Using integrated GPS capability in conjunction with its existing inertial navigation computer system the missile has exceptional accuracy.

The AGM-86C carries a HE blast/fragmentation warhead while the AGM-86D (50 converted) has avionics upgrades and a new, penetrating warhead for use against hardened and buried targets. During 20 years of operational service over 200 AGM-86Cs have been launched in various regional conflicts, demonstrating the weapon's ability to deliver a large conventional warhead with exceptional accuracy over distances of 600-700nm.

BGM-109 Tomahawk

Manufacturer: Raytheon, USA.

Type: Long-range submarine/ship-launched cruise missile.

Weight: 2,650lb (1,193kg); 3,200lb (1,440kg) with booster.

Dimensions: Length with booster 20.5ft (6.3m); length without booster
18.3ft (5.6m); diameter 20.4in (51.8cm); wing span 8.8ft (2.7m).

Powerplant: Williams International F107-WR-402 cruise turbo-fan engine; solid-fuel booster.

Performance: Maximum speed about 550mph (880km/h); range (land attack,
conventional warhead) 600nm (690 statute miles/1,104km).

Guidance: Inertial and TERCOM.

Warhead: (All conventional) 1,000lb (454kg) Bullpup, or submunitions
dispenser with combined effect bomblets, or WDU-36 warhead.

▲ **Above**   *Tomahawk emerges from the depths, launched by a hidden SSN.*

The Tomahawk land-attack cruise missile has a solid-propellant booster, which accelerates it to cruise speed, whereupon a small turbofan engine takes over and the booster is jettisoned. Tomahawk is extremely hard to detect by hostile radar, due to its very small radar cross-section and low-altitude flight profile, while infrared detection is also very difficult as a result of careful design combined with the low heat emissions of its turbojet engine.

Following the Gulf War, the Navy took steps to improve Tomahawk's operational responsiveness, target penetration, range, and accuracy, the outcome being the Block III system upgrade, which includes jam-resistant Global Positioning System (GPS) receivers, freeing the guidance system from its dependence on terrain features. The new warhead has a more powerful explosive and more responsive fuzing systems. Block III missiles were first used in the September 1995 against targets in Bosnia and a year later against Iraq.

▲ **Above**   *Tomahawk launched from a surface warship. These missiles had a devastating effect in the 1991 war, their pin-point accuracy and destructive terminal effects coming as a major shock to Iraqi commanders.*

BOMBERS

Concurrent with the cruise missiles, the initial US attacks will be carried out by manned bombers, of which the USAF operates three quite distinct types: the venerable, but still highly effective B-52, the swing-wing B-1B and the ultra-stealthy B-2. Most of these aircraft will operate from the US base on the British island of Diego Garcia, thus cutting out the long approach flights of previous campaigns. They have different flight characteristics, but one thing in common is that they are all very difficult, if not impossible targets for the Iraqis, who have no missiles or fighter aircraft capable of attacking them.

Although bombers do not fight other bombers, the comparison with the Iraqi bomber "force" is very striking. In the 1980s the Iraqis operated several Tu-16s supplied by the USSR and four Xian H-6s, a PRC version of the same aircraft, together with some 4-6 Tu-22 supersonic bombers. Of these, perhaps 2-3 H-6s survive.

	Country	Weight	Range	Bombload	Number in service
B-52H	USA	488,000lb	8,800nm	70,000lb	57
B-1B	USA	477,000lb	6,475nm	134,000lb	91
B-2	USA	376,000lb	6,300nm	40,000lb	20
Xian H-6	Iraq	169,755lb	2,980nm	19,841lb	2-3

US/IRAQI Bombers: A comparison

B-52H Stratofortress

Manufacturer: Boeing, USA.

Type: Strategic bomber.

Weight: Empty, approx. 185,000lb (83,250kg); max takeoff 488,000lb (219,600kg).

Dimensions: Length 159.1ft (48.5m); height 40.7ft (12.4m); wingspan 185.0ft (56.4m);

Powerplant: Eight Pratt & Whitney TF33-P-3/103 turbofans, each 17,000lb (7,711kg) thrust.

Performance: Speed 650mph (1,040km/h, Mach 0.86); ceiling 49,712ft (15,152m); unrefueled range, 8,800 miles (7,652nm, 14,080km).

▲ **Above**   *Most B-52H bombers will operate from Diego Garcia island, less than 3,000 miles from Iraq.*

Armament: Approx. 70,000lb (31,500kg) mixed ordnance, bombs, mines, air-launched cruise missiles, Harpoon anti-ship and Have Nap missiles.

Crew: Five (commander, co-pilot, radar navigator, navigator and electronic warfare officer), with six ejection seats.

B-52s have recently been seen on TVs across the world dropping bombs on targets in Afghanistan with great precision, and they will do so again against Iraq. All aircraft now in service are the B-52H, the last of which was delivered in October 1962; these carry up to 20 air-launched cruise missiles, or large numbers of bombs of various types. All are equipped with numerous electronic systems, including a comprehensive electronic countermeasures (ECM) suite. One of the most recent additions is the electro-optical viewing system using forward-looking infrared (FLIR) and high resolution low-light-level television (LLTV) to augment targeting, battle assessment, and flight safety, thus further improving the bomber's combat ability and low-level flight capability. During night operations pilots wear night vision goggles to enable them to clear terrain, avoid enemy radar and see other aircraft in a covert/lights-out environment. Unrefueled combat range is in excess of 8,800 miles, but with aerial refueling range is limited only by crew endurance.

B-1B Lancer

Manufacturer: Boeing (Rockwell), USA.

Type: Strategic bomber.

Weight: Empty approx. 190,000lb (86,183kg); max takeoff 477,000lb (216,367kg).

Dimensions: Length 146.0ft (44.5m); height 34.0ft (10.4m); wingspan, wings forward 136.7ft (41.7m), wings swept 78.2ft (23.8m).

Powerplant: Four General Electric F-101-GE-102 turbofans, each of 30,000lb (13,600kg)+ thrust with afterburner.

Performance: Speed (sea level) 900mph (1,440km/h, Mach 1.25); range approx. 6,475nm (12,000km) unrefueled; ceiling >30,000ft (9,144m).

Armament: Three internal weapons bays accommodating up to 84 Mk-82 general purpose bombs or Mk-62 naval mines, 30 CBU-87/89 cluster munitions or CBU-97 Sensor Fuzed Weapons and up to 24 GBU-31 JDAM GPS guided bombs or Mk-84 general purpose bombs.

Crew: Four (commander, co-pilot, offensive systems officer and defensive systems officer).

The B-1B has a very low radar cross-section (RCS), reportedly one-hundredth that of the B-52. Its ability to deliver conventional weapons is being constantly improved, the latest upgrade to be completed being the Conventional Mission Upgrade Program (CMUP) Block D which enables aircraft to carry 24 JDAM guided bombs and to tow an Integrated Defensive Electronic CounterMeasures (IDECM) decoy to enhance the survivability of the aircraft. There is also a new communication/navigation system.

The B-1B was designed to fly low-level, high-speed missions which impose greater strain on the airframe than the high-altitude missions of the B-52. The last of 100 aircraft was delivered in May 1988, since when the type has equipped three squadrons of Air Combat Command, and two of the Air National Guard. There are currently 51 primary mission aircraft in the active inventory (72 actual), and 18 with the ANG (20 actual), and a further two aircraft are used in test programs. Each airframe is expected to have a 10,000 hour service life, allowing it to remain in service until around 2020, when, like the B-2, it will retire long before the much older B-52.

The aircraft was first used in combat in support of operations against Iraq during Operation Desert Fox in December 1998 and has subsequently been used in Operation Allied Force in the Former Yugoslavia and in Afghanistan in 2001/2002.

▼ **Below**   *Loading weapons into a B-1B Lancer. There are 92 in the inventory: 72 with the USAF, 20 with the Air National Guard and 2 in trials programs. Of these, 69 are normally operational, but more would be available in an emergency.*

B-2A Spirit

Manufacturer: Northrop Grumman, USA

Type: Strategic bomber.

Weight: Empty, 153,700 lb (69,717kg); normal take-off, 336,500lb (152,600kg); max take-off, 376,000lb (170,550kg).

Dimensions: Length 69ft (20.9m); height 17ft (5.2m); wingspan 172ft (52.4m).

Powerplant: Four General Electric F118-GE-100 turbofans, each of 17,300lb (7,850kg) thrust.

Performance: Max. speed high subsonic (approx Mach 0.85); ceiling: 50,000ft (15,000m); range (typical, hi-hi-hi): 6,300nm (11,667km).

Armament: 40,000lb (18,000kg) of ordnance in internal bays.

Crew: Two (pilot, co-pilot/mission commander).

The B-2A achieved Initial Operational Capability (IOC) in April 1997, with 21 aircraft stationed at the type's only base, Whiteman AFB. The first 16 aircraft were delivered to the Block 1 standard and were armed with B83 or Mk 84 nuclear weapons, while the next three (#17-#19) were built to Block 2 standard, following which #12-#16 were retrofitted to the same standard. Block 2 equipped the aircraft with partial terrain-following capability, the GATS (GPS-Aided Targeting System), which allowed it to operate from forward bases. A minor modification, Block 20, enabled aircraft to deliver 16 Joint Direct Attack Munitions (JDAMs). The final aircraft, #20 and #21 (the rebuilt #1), were completed to Block 30 standard, to which the other 19 will be upgraded. Block 30 has full low-observability performance, full JDAM launch capability, and can carry up to 80 Mk 82, 36 M117 or 80 Mk 62 bombs.

▲ **Above**   *The stealthy B-2 Spirit has proved a highly effective bomber, capable of delivering a large load of a variety of conventional weapons over long ranges.*

H-6 (Tupolev Tu-16) (NATO = Badger)

Manufacturer: Xian, China.

Type: Strategic bomber/ maritime strike.

Weights: Empty 92,5901b (42t), maximum loaded 169,7551b (77t).

Dimensions: Length 114ft 2in (34.2m); height 35ft 51n (10.8m); wingspan 112ft 2in (34.2m).

Powerplant: Two Xian Wopen-8 (Mikulin RD-3M) turbojets; 20,9501b (9.5t) thrust.

Performance: Maximum speed (30,000ft/9,000m) 587mph (945km/h); long-range cruise 485mph (780km/h); service ceiling 42,650ft (13km); range with missile/bomb load about 2,980 miles (4,8000km).

Armament: Maximum bombs 19,841lb (9,000kg); or two C-801 anti-ship missiles.

Crew: Six.

The PRC exported four Xian H-6Ds to Iraq in the mid-1980s and even if only one or two remain airworthy they pose a threat to US forces. Developed from the Soviet Tu-16 Badger, the H-6 is one of the largest twin-engined bombers in history. The -D version is basically a maritime surveillance and missile-guidance platform, with large nose and chin radars, and three ventral aerial fairings. In PRC service it can carry either a free-fall nuclear weapon, a number of conventional bombs, or two C-801 anti-ship missiles on underwing launch rails.

The four Iraqi H-6Ds were not among the aircraft that fled to Iran in 1991 and one possible scenario in which they might be used is in a suicidal "final" mission as the Saddam regime faces extinction, in which they would deliver conventional bombs or chemical/ biological weapons against a high-value target somewhere in the Middle East. Alternatively, they might be used with their anti-ship missiles to attack a US Navy carrier in the Gulf.

▼ **Below** *Very few Tu-16-derived Xian H-6 bombers may be available to Iraq, but how they might be used is not known. When all is lost, Saddam may persuade fanatical followers to launch a suicide attack on a high value US/Israeli target.*

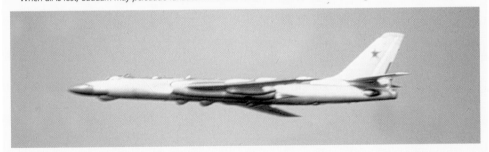

STRIKE AIRCRAFT

The United States' bomber onslaught will be complemented by attack aircraft, hitting targets in support of the operational and tactical plans. US strike aircraft assets include the Air Force's F-117 Nighthawk and F-16 Fighting Falcon, the Marines' AV-8 Harrier, and the F/A-18 Hornet, which is operated by both the Navy and the Marines. First into the fray will be the F-117 Nighthawk, of which the USAF currently operates a fleet of 54. These have flown in the former Yugoslavia and in the first Gulf War, where their weapons proved particularly effective against Iraqi Air Force hardened air shelters.

The general missions of the American strike aircraft will include air superiority, close and deep air support, fighter escort, forward air control, suppression of enemy air defenses (SEAD), reconnaissance, and strike missions by both day and night.

The frustration for the Iraqi strike aircraft pilots will be that, as in the 1991 Gulf War, there will be a multitude of American targets scattered across the countryside, but they will have very little possibility of being able to attack them. Their assets are very slender, a small number of Sukhoi Su-22s, Chengdu F-7s and Dassault Mirage F1s, but these aircraft and their airfields will be among the very first priority targets in the opening phase of the United States air campaign.

F-117A Nighthawk

Manufacturer: Lockheed Martin, USA.

Type: Single-seat, single-engined strike fighter.

Weight: Empty approx 30,000lb (13,610kg); maximum take-off 52,500lb (23,800kg)

Dimensions: Length 65ft 11in (20.1m); height 12ft 5in (3.8m); wingspan 43ft 4in (13.2m).

Powerplant: Two General Electric F404-GE-F1D2 turbofans (non-afterburning), each approximately 10,800lb static thrust (48.0kN).

Performance: Max level speed, high altitude, clean condition >Mach 1.0, at optimum altitude approx Mach 0.9; combat radius with max ordnance approx 600nm (690 miles/1,110km).

Armament: Approx 5,000lb (2,270kg) ordnance (all internal).

Crew: One.

F-117s played a key role in the Coalition victory over Iraq in 1991 and will do so again in 2003. This unique aircraft keeps radar cross-section (RCS) to a minimum using flat panels and straight lines rather than the traditional curves. Also, these panels are coated with radar-absorbent materials and are mounted on a skeletal sub-frame. The cockpit canopy and most access panels have serrated edges to suppress radar reflection, while the rectangular engine intakes are covered by slotted screens to prevent radar energy entering. All ordnance is carried internally. Despite its title "stealth fighter," the F-117A is essentially a strike aircraft designed to approach its target at subsonic speed, launch a missile or "smart" bomb and then turn away for its return to base. It would be no match for a traditional fighter in terms of speed or agility and to avoid such confrontations, it normally operates at night, when it is virtually undetectable.

Some 42 F-117As took part in Desert Storm, when they regularly attacked targets in and around Baghdad and then elsewhere in the country, eventually flying a total of 1,271 missions. All F-117As are concentrated in Air Combat Command's 49th Fighter Wing (formerly the 4450th Tactical Group) which currently has 54 aircraft on strength.

▼ **Below** *A pair of F-117As prepare to take off on a nocturnal mission. Such stealth strike aircraft are almost impossible for the Iraqis to counter and will be in the first wave of attack, just as they were in the 1991 Gulf War.*

F/A-18C/D Hornet/Super Hornet

Manufacturer: Boeing (McDonnell Douglas), USA.

Type: Multi-role attack and fighter aircraft.

Weight: Empty 23,050lb (10,455kg); normal take-off, fighter mission 36,710lb (16,652kg); normal take-off, attack mission 51,900lb (23,537kg).

Dimensions: Length 56.0ft (16.8m); height 15.3ft (4.6m); wingspan 40.4ft (13.5m).

Powerplant: Two F404-GE-402 turbofans, each 16,700lb (78.7kN) with afterburning.

Performance: Max level speed at high altitude, clean >1,033kt (1,190mph/1,915km/h); ceiling: >50,000ft (15,240m); range with external tanks, fighter, 1,379nm (1586miles/2,537km); attack, 1,333nm (1533miles/ 2,453km).

Armament: One M61A1/A2 Vulcan 20mm cannon; external, combinations of AIM-9 Sidewinder, AIM-7 Sparrow, AIM-120 Amraam; Harpoon, HARM, Shrike, SLAM, SLAM-ER, Walleye, Maverick missiles; Joint Stand-Off Weapon (JSOW); Joint Direct Attack Munition (JDAM); general purpose bombs, mines and rockets.

Crew: F/A-18C – one; F/A-18D – two.

▲ **Above** *The latest Hornet, an F/A-18F two-seater on final approach to a carrier landing. The -E/-F versions have greatly improved mission range and endurance compared to earlier models of this outstanding airplane.*

Large numbers of F/A-18s will be at the forefront of Navy and Marine Corps participation in the war against Iraq. The F/A-18 is a true multi-mission platform, It uses a digital fly-by-wire control system which gives excellent handling, enables pilots to convert to the type with relative ease, and also makes it an exceptionally manoeuvrable aircraft, able to hold its own against any adversary.

The F/A-18E/F "Super Hornet," now entering service, is 4.2ft (1.3m) longer than earlier Hornets, with new engines, a 25 percent increase in wing area and a 33 percent increase in internal fuel, all of which combine to give a 41 percent increase in mission range and a 50 percent increase in endurance. The F/A-18E/F has 11 weapons stations: two on the wing tips for missiles, six underwing stations (three per wing) for air-to-ground weapons or fuel tanks, two fuselage stations for Sparrows or sensor pods, and a centerline station for fuel or air-to-ground weapons. Finally, as in earlier versions, a 20mm M61A1 Vulcan cannon is mounted internally in the nose.

AV-8B Harrier II and Harrier II Plus

Manufacturer: Boeing, USA/British Aerospace, UK.

Type: Vertical/short takeoff and landing attack aircraft.

Weight: Normal take-off 22,950lb (10,410kg); max short take-off 31,000lb (14,061kg); max vertical take-off 18,950lb (8,595kg).

Dimensions: Length 46ft 4in (14.1m); height 11ft 5in (3.6m); wingspan 30ft 4in (9.3m).

▲ **Above** *US Marine Corps AV-8B leaves USS Peleliu for Afghanistan.*

Powerplant: One Rolls-Royce Pegasus F-402-RR-408, 21,500lb (9,751kg) dry thrust.

Performance: Max level speed, clean, sea level 661mph (1,065km/h); range, ferry 2,418nm (3891km); combat radius (12 x Mk82 bombs, 1 hour loiter, STO) 103nm (167km); max rate of climb at sea level 14,715ft/min (4,485m); service ceiling approx 50,000ft (15,240m).

Armament: One fuselage-mounted 25mm gun system. Typical ordnance loads are six Mk 82 500lb bombs, or four AIM-9L/M Sidewinder missiles; maximum ordnance 9,200lb (4,173kg).

Crew: One

Primary missions of the Marines' AV-8Bs are to support ground troops and escort helicopters, but they can be given other missions by the relevant commander. AV-8Bs can operate from any appropriate sea or land platform/base, and are capable of air-to-air refueling.

During Operation Desert Storm, AV-8Bs were the first U.S. Marine Corps tactical aircraft to arrive in theater, where they operated from an unused airfield and a small forward-based airstrip, as well as from ships in the Persian Gulf. The 86 AV-8Bs involved were in combat for 42 days, during which they flew 3,380 combat sorties, delivering over six million pounds of ordnance during 4,112 hours of combat flying. Over the entire period of Desert Storm, AV-8B squadrons achieved an aircraft readiness rate greater than 90 percent.

◀ **Left** *AV-8B launches an AGM-65E Maverick laser-guided missile.*

F-16 Fighting Falcon

Manufacturer: Lockheed Martin (General Dynamics), USA.

Type: Single-seat air superiority and multi-role fighter.

Weight: Empty 19,020lb (8,627kg); normal takeoff 28,500lb (12,928kg); max 2,300lb (19,187kg).

Dimensions: Length 49ft 4in (15.0m); height 16ft 10in (5.1m); wingspan 32ft 6in (9.8m).

Powerplant: One General Electric F110-GE-100 afterburning turbofan rated at 28,982lb (13,146kg) max thrust.

Performance: Max speed 1,500mph (Mach 2) at altitude, Mach 1.2 at sea level; initial climb rate 50,000ft/min (254m/sec); ceiling > 50,000ft (15,000m); operational radius 490 miles (788km); ferry range > 2,000 miles.

Armament: One M-61A1 20mm six-barrel cannon with 511 rounds; external stations can carry up to six AIM-9 Sidewinders, AIM 120 Amraam, R550 Magic 2, MICA, or Python 3 AAMs, or in combination.

Crew: One.

F-16 multi-role fighters have proved their worth in numerous campaigns. In air combat the F-16's maneuverability and combat radius exceed those of all potential threat fighter aircraft. It can locate targets in all weather conditions and it can detect low-flying aircraft in radar ground clutter. In its air-to-surface role, the F-16 can fly more than 500nm (860km), deliver its weapons with great accuracy, even during non-visual bombing conditions, defend itself against attack by enemy aircraft, and then return to base.

USAF F-16 multi-mission fighters were deployed in the 1991 Gulf War, where they flew more sorties than any other type, attacking airfields, military production facilities, Scud missile sites and many other targets. More recently, during Operation Allied Force in 1999, F-16s flew suppression of enemy air defense (SEAD), offensive/defensive counter air, close air support and forward air controller missions.

▼ **Below** *A load of "iron bombs" being released by an F-16 Fighting Falcon. This capable aircraft can drop a wide variety of weapons, then defend itself against hostile fighters.*

Su-22 (NATO = Fitter)

Manufacturer: Sukhoi, USSR.

Type: Ground-attack fighter.

Weights: Empty 22,500lb (10,200kg); max loaded 42,330lb (19,200kg).

Dimensions: Length 50ft 6in (15.8m); height 16ft 5in (5.0m); wingspan (28 degree wing sweep) 45ft 11in (14.0m), (62 degree wing sweep) 34ft 9in (10.6m).

Powerplant: One Lyulka Al-21F-21 afterburning turbojet, 17,200/24,700lb (7.8/11.2t).

Performance: Max speed (clean, typical) at sea level 800mph (1,290km/h, Mach 1.05), at 36,000ft (10,970m) 1,435mph (2,300km/h, Mach 2.2); service ceiling 59,050ft (18km).

Armament: Two NR-30 cannon (each 70 rounds) and two Atoll/Aphid AAM, eight pylons for total of 8,820lb (4,0000kg) external ordnance/tanks.

Crew: One.

One of the most numerous aircraft types remaining with the Iraqi Air Force is this ground-attack fighter, the Soviet Union having supplied several hundred Su-20 (NATO = Fitter-C) and Su-22 (NATO = Fitter-G). Some 44 of these fled to Iran in 1991, while many others were destroyed on the ground by Coalition attacks. However, at least 40 are estimated to survive, and the numbers may possibly be greater, although serviceability is likely to be low.

▼ **Below** *Some of the several hundred Sukhoi Su-22s supplied to Iraq should still be operational, but whether their pilots are prepared to fly them in the face of overwhelming US air superiority is another matter.*

F-7B/MiG-21

Manufacturer: Chengdu, China/MiG, USSR.

Type: Fighter (some fighter/bomber or reconnaissance).

Weight: Empty 12,440lb (5,643kg); loaded (50 percent fuel/two missiles) 15,000lb (6,800kg); max 20,725lb (9,400kg).

Dimensions: Length 44ft 2in (13.46m); height 13ft 6in (4.2m); wingspan 23ft 6in (7.2m).

Powerplant: F-7B – one Liyang Wopen WP-7B 13,488lb (6,118kg) static thrust with afterburning; MiG-21 – Tumanskiy R-11 afterburning turbojet 13,120lb (5,951kg) static thrust.

Performance: Max speed (sea level) 800mph (1,290km/h, Mach 1.05), (36,000ft/ 11,000m, clean) 1,385mph (2,230km/h, Mach 2.1); initial climb about 30,000ft (9,144m)/min; practical ceiling about 50,000ft (15,240m); range, internal fuel 395 miles (632km), with three tanks 695 miles (1,112km).

Armament: Two NR-30 cannon, two pylons for KI 3A AAMs or UV-16-57 rockets, (later models) one GP-9 belly pack containing GSh-23 cannon with 200 rounds and four wing pylons for missiles, bombs, rockets or drop tanks.

Crew: One.

Built in larger numbers than any other modern combat aircraft, the Russian MiG-21 began life as a very high performance interceptor, but somewhat deficient in weapons and avionics. The Chengdu J-7 was built in the PRC, initially as a direct copy of an early MiG-21. Since then it has been developed by Chinese designers both for the PRC air force and also for export as the F-7. About 80 F-7Bs were exported to Iraq in the 1980s.

None of the reports of the Iraqi aircraft flown to Iran in January 1991 included any mention of either MiG-21s or F-7Bs, so it must be assumed that of the 180-odd delivered, some would have been destroyed by Coalition air forces during the Gulf War, but the majority may well have survived. Current estimates are that some 40-50 remain in service, but how airworthy they are is unknown.

▲ *Above*   *China has supplied a large number of aircraft to Iraq, including the F-7, some 80 of which were delivered in the 1980s. This is a PRC-developed version of the widely used MiG-21 air defense fighter.*

Mirage F1EQ

Manufacturer: Dassault, France.

Type: Single-seat multimission fighter.

Weight: Empty 17,857lb (8100kg); loaded (clean) 25,450lb (11,540kg), (max) 33,510lb (15,200kg).

Dimensions: Length 50ft 11in (15.53m), height 14ft 10in (4.56m); wingspan 27ft 6in (84m).

Powerplant: One SNECMA M53-02 single-shaft augmented by-pass turbojet, 18,740lb (85,00kg) thrust (max afterburner).

Performance: Max speed (clean) 915mph (1,472km/h, Mach 1.2); rate of climb >59,000ft (18,000m)/min; service ceiling 69,750ft (21,250m), range loaded (hi-lo-hi) 621 miles (1,000km), (ferry range) 2,340 miles (3,765km).

Armament: Two 30mm DEFA 5-53 cannon (each 135 rounds); typical air combat weapons, two Matra 550 Magic or Sidewinder, one/two Matra 530.

Crew: One.

In 1967 the French engine company, SNECMA, began the design of a completely new engine for the Super Mirage, for which a Mirage F1E was used as a test-bed. However, this combination proved of interest in its own right, since the M53 engine conferred benefits in acceleration, climb, maneuverability and range. The outcome was the F1E, of which Iraq ordered 110 aircraft, designated F-1EQ, although only 93 were actually delivered. The Iraqi Air Force also took delivery of 15 F1BQ two-seat trainer aircraft. At least one of these has been tested as a chemical agent sprayer.

▲ **Above**   The Mirage F1EQ is an effective, if somewhat dated, French-built fighter. At least one is known to have been used by the Iraqis as a testbed for biological agent delivery system, a very ominous development.

AIRBORNE COMMAND-AND-CONTROL AND ELECTRONIC WARFARE AIRCRAFT

Modern military operations require sophisticated command and control, and if the United States is somewhat in advance of Iraq in some respects, it is light years ahead in airborne electronic systems. The E-3 AWACS and E-8 Joint STARS both provide surveillance, information gathering and control facilities, and have proved themselves in the 1991 Gulf War and regional conflicts since, and have been subjected to repeated upgrading throughout their operational lives. Both ensure that the control of friendly air and land assets is maximized to identify and designate enemy positions and equipment and then to bring maximum force to bear to neutralize or destroy them.

The Iraqis did, in fact, make an attempt to produce an AWACS aircraft by converting two Soviet-supplied Ilyushin Il-76 to the role. Designated "Adnan," neither survived the 1991 Gulf War.

The United States also operates a wide variety of electronic warfare aircraft, all of them specialized conversions of aircraft originally designed for other roles. The USAF has a large number of EW conversions of KC-135s and C-130s, while the Navy has its own fleet of converted Lockheed P-3 Orions and the Army its RC-12 Guardrail aircraft. There are also a number of Grumman E-6 Prowlers, originally Navy/Marine aircraft but now operated as joint-service assets. The EC-130H Compass Call described below is just one representative of a large number of such aircraft.

Although visually unexciting and lacking the dramatic appearance of a fighter or a bomber, the influence of EW aircraft must never be underestimated. The fighting in the electronic battlefield is as unremitting and as vicious as anything involving the physical use of weapons, and can have as much, sometimes even more, effect on the outcome of the war. Thus, great numbers of these aircraft will be very active in the skies overlooking Iraq, waging their own wars in the virtual battleground of the electronic spectrum.

E-3 Sentry

Manufacturer: Boeing, USA.
Type: Airborne warning and control system (AWACS).
Weight: Max take-off 347,000lb (156,150kg).
Dimensions: Length 145ft 6in (44.0m); height 41ft 4in (12.5m); wingspan130ft 7in (39.7m). Radome – diameter 30ft 0in (9.1m); depth 6ft 0in (1.8m).
Powerplant: Four Pratt & Whitney TF33-PW-100A turbofans, each 21,000lb (9,450kg) static thrust.
Performance: Optimum cruising 360mph (Mach 0.48); ceiling approx 29,000ft (8,788m); endurance, internal fuel >11 hours.
Armament: None.
Crew: 21 (four flight crew, 13-19 AWACS mission specialists).

◀ **Left** The E-3's huge, electronics-packed rotating radome is 30 feet in diameter and 6 feet deep.

Continued over

The E-3's disc-shaped radome houses a Westinghouse AN/APY-2 radar, providing surveillance coverage to 250 miles (375km) for low-flying targets and much further for aircraft flying at medium to high altitudes. The radar includes an Identification Friend or Foe (IFF) sub-system and these sensors, in conjunction with a powerful computer, enable the operators to perform real-time surveillance, identification, weapons control, battle management and communications functions. Tracks are classified as land, air or sea, friendly or hostile, while data downlinks enable all information to be passed to command centers in rear areas or aboard ships, or, in time of crisis, to the National Command Authorities. Missions normally last for some 8-10 hours, but air-to-air refueling and on-board rest facilities give much greater endurance. E-3s are among the first assets to be deployed in any crisis and in Operation Desert Shield/Desert Storm they flew more than 400 missions, logging more than 5,000 hours of on-station time, providing radar surveillance and control for more than 120,000 Coalition sorties.

▲ **Above** *A USAF E-3 takes off on a vital mission. The whole concept of an airborne early warning and command system revolutionized the way the US Air Force controlled the air battle.*

E-8C Joint STARS

Manufacturer: Northrop Grumman, USA.

Type: Airborne battle management.

Weight: Empty 171,000lb (77,565kg); with max fuel 336,000lb (152,408kg).

Dimensions: Length 152ft 11in (46.6m); height 42ft 6in (13.0m); wingspan 145ft 10in (44.4m).

Powerplant: Four Pratt & Whitney TF33-102C; each 19,000lb (8,618kg) static thrust.

Performance: Max cruising speed at 25,000ft (7,620m) 525kt (605mph/973km/h); optimum orbiting speed (depending on altitude) 390-510kt (Mach 0.52-0.65); ceiling 42,000ft (12,800m); range with max fuel 5,000nm (5,758 miles/9,266km); endurance, unrefueled 11 hours, refueled 20 hours.

Armament: None.

Crew: Standard mission, 21 (flightcrew – 3; mission crew – Army 3, Air Force 15; protracted mission 34 (flightcrew 6, mission operators 28).

The Joint Surveillance Target Attack Radar System (Joint STARS) is an Air Force-Army program consisting of an airborne element – an E-8C, a converted Boeing 707 aircraft with a multi-mode radar system – and a ground element of Army-operated, vehicle-mounted Ground Station Modules (GSMs). The aircraft carries a phased-array radar antenna, providing targeting and battle management data to all Joint STARS operators, both in the aircraft and on the ground, who then call on aircraft, missiles or artillery for fire support. The radar has a range greater than 155 miles (250km) and covers some 386,100sq miles (1,000,000sq km) in a single eight-hour sortie, and detects, locates and identifies slow-moving targets, differentiating between wheeled and tracked vehicles. The Synthetic Aperture Radar/Fixed Target Indicator (SAR/FTI) produces data maps showing the precise locations of critical stationary targets such as bridges, harbors, airports, buildings, or vehicles.

▼ **Below** *E-8 Joint STARS was rushed into service during the 1991 Gulf War and proved an immediate success, bringing a new dimension to control of some aspects of the land battle, particularly fire support.*

EC-130H Compass Call/Rivet Fire

Manufacturer: Lockheed Martin, USA.

Type: Tactical command, control and communications countermeasures (C3CM).

Weight: Empty 69,300lb (31,434kg); max take-off 135,000lb (61,236kg).

Dimensions: Length 97ft 9in (29.3m); height 38ft 4in (11.4m); wingspan 132ft 7in (39.7m).

Powerplant: Four Rolls-Royce Allison T56-A-15 turboprops; each 4,300shp (3,080kW).

Performance: Max cruising speed 321kt (370mph/595km/h) at 30,000ft (9,144m); range 4,210nm (4,848 miles/7,802km) with max fuel or 1,910nm (2,199 miles/3,539km) with max payload.

Armament: None.

Crew: 13 (two pilots, navigator, flight engineer, plus nine specialist operators).

EC-130H Compass Call is typical of the many electronic warfare versions of the C-130, which in this case is adapted for use as a tactical command, control and communications countermeasures (C3CM) platform, mounting electronic attacks on hostile command-and-control systems. Such support gives friendly commanders an immense advantage before and during the air campaign. Compass Call is known to use noise jamming to prevent communications and degrade transfer of information essential to command and control of weapon systems and other resources. Although the aircraft's primary mission is in support of tactical air operations, it can also provide jamming support to ground force operations.

Modifications to the aircraft include an electronic countermeasures system (Rivet Fire), and air refueling capability. External indications of the aircraft's role are two blisters, one each side of the rear fuselage, and a gantry under the tail which is used to deploy wire antennas. There are 13 aircraft in total, with five in each of two squadrons and three as attrition reserves.

▲ **Above** *C-130 airframes are used for many special purposes, such as this USAF EC-130H Compass Call, 10 of which are currently in the inventory. Note the special antennas under the wings and forward of the rudder.*

U-2S

Manufacturer: Lockheed Martin, USA.
Type: High-altitude reconnaissance.
Weight: Max take-off 40,000lb (18,140kg).
Dimensions: Length 63ft 0in (19.2m);
height 16ft 0in (4.9m); wingspan
103ft 0in (31.4m).
Powerplant: One General Electric
F-118-101 turbofan, 17,000lb (7,710kg)
static thrust.
Performance: Max speed >475mph
(Mach 0.58); ceiling >70,000ft
(21,212m); range >
6,000nm (11,280km).
Armament: None.
Crew: One.

▲ **Above**   *The high-flying U-2S provides surveillance coverage unmatched by any other platform.*

One of the most famous reconnaissance aircraft in aviation history, the U-2S plays a crucial role in modern operations; it flew missions over Iraq in 1990-91, and will fly many more during the coming conflict. The original U-2 was designed to overfly the Soviet Union at heights of over 70,000ft (21,000m), but in the early 1990s the entire fleet was upgraded by installing the General Electric F118-GE-101 turbofan engine, which was lighter, produced more thrust, and burned less fuel than the original J75. Designated U-2S, this aircraft collects multi-sensor photographic, electro-optical, infrared and radar imagery, as well as performing other types of reconnaissance.

Its high aspect ratio wings give the U-2 glider-like flying characteristics and make the aircraft extremely challenging to control in certain regimes, especially when landing, while the high-altitude mission means that the pilot must wear a full pressure suit, which adds to the challenge of flying the aircraft. There are currently 35 aircraft in the Air Force inventory, of which four are two-seat trainers.

TRANSPORT AND TANKER AIRCRAFT

The United States' air transport fleet is also large, ranging from 109 of the huge C-5 Galaxy through over 500 C-130s down to a handful of the tiny C-12 SuperKings. Even with these great resources, however, the government still has to turn to the Civil Reserve Air Fleet and commercial contractors for additional capacity when major operations are in progress. By comparison, the Iraqis have a few military transport aircraft and would doubtless requisition commercial aircraft, but the numbers are very small and the chances of survival in the face of US air supremacy very slight.

To give some idea of the scale of the US airlift capabilities, during Operation Desert Shield in 1990, in little more than a month from the order to begin, American airlift aircraft moved more men and materiel into the Gulf than had gone to Southeast Asia in the first eight months of the Vietnam War. One just one day, 29 August, Dover AFB dispatched more than 1,000,000lb (453,000kg) of cargo to the Gulf. By the end of September, US commercial aircraft had already flown more than 500 missions, delivering some 66,000 personnel and 5,000,000lb (2,270,000kg) of cargo, with up to 40 airliners taking part each day. The efforts and skills of those organizing distribution on the ground is also one of the great unsung stories of the war.

Flight-refueling operations will be of even more importance to US air assets during the coming war with Iraq, especially in the light of probable limits on overflying of neighboring countries. During Desert Shield and Desert Storm, such operations were the largest ever undertaken. Then, tankers used to support the first US fighters to reach the area were available to fly operations from Saudi Arabia within 24 hours of arrival, and more than 8,500 sorties had been flown by mid-February 1991. Such was the pace of Gulf operations that a tanker squadron could clock up more sorties during the war than most would undertake in a year of peacetime training operations.

▲ **Above**   A C-141 transport delivers paratroops on a tactical mission.

▲ **Above**   A US general once said that war depended on "getting there firstest with the mostest," a mission in which the massive air transport fleet plays a key role. This USAF C-5 delivers a SEALs Mark V patrol boat, a load it lifts with ease.

C-5A Galaxy

Manufacturer: Lockheed-Martin, USA.

Type: Strategic troop and cargo carrier.

Weight: Operating empty 374,000lb (169,643kg); max takeoff, peacetime 769,000lb (348,818kg), wartime 840,000lb (381,024kg).

Dimensions: Length 247ft 10in (75.3m); height 65ft 2in (19.8m); wingspan 222ft 11in (67.9 m).

Powerplant: Four General Electric TF-39GE-1C turbofans; each 43,000lb (19,500kg) static thrust.

Performance: Max speed 402kt (463mph/741km/h); max cruising speed at 25,000ft (7,620m) 480kt (578mph/930km/h)); range empty with max fuel 5,618nm (6,469 miles/10,411km).

Payload: Max wartime 291,000lb (130,950kg) (see notes).

Crew: Seven (pilot, co-pilot, two flight engineers and three loadmasters).

▲ **Above**   The C-5 has massive doors at both ends of the fuselage, enabling big weapons, such as two M1 battle tanks, or a CH-47 helicopter to be loaded and unloaded with ease, even at a relatively small airfield.

The Lockheed C-5 Galaxy provides air transport on a massive scale, with a cargo hold 13.5ft (4.1m) high, 19.0ft (5.8m) wide and 143.8ft (43.8m) long and full-size doors at each end which not only enable huge loads to be accommodated, but also allow ground crews to work at both ends simultaneously. The undercarriage also has a special "kneeling" facility to bring the aircraft sill down to the level of a truck bed. In addition, 73 passengers can be accommodated on the upper deck and a further 14 on the forward upper deck, plus a relief crew of seven. The hauling capacity of the C-5 is enormous. It can accommodate two M1 tanks, an Armored Vehicle Launched Bridge (AVLB), ten of the Marine Corps LAV-25s, or a Ch-47 Chinook helicopter.

A total of 77 C-5As were built, but an increased demand for heavy-lift capacity led to the line being reopened for the production of 50 C-5Bs between 1986 and 1989. The C-5B incorporates many enhancements, not least a greatly simplified version of the 28-wheel undercarriage. An updating program began in the 1990s. This has included avionics modernization and reliability enhancement, the latter including replacement of the engines, pods and auxiliary power units. Like the C-17 and C-141, the C-5 is capable of conducting clandestine flights into potentially hostile territory to either airdrop or airland troops, equipment or both. These aircraft are fitted with SOLL-II (Special Operations Low-Level - Image Intensifier) which enables them to operate in darkness. The current inventory is 70 C-5s with the Active force, 11 with the Air National Guard and 28 with the Air Force Reserve.

C-17 Globemaster III

Manufacturer: Boeing (McDonnell Douglas), USA.
Type: Strategic/tactical cargo/troop transport.
Weight: Max peacetime take-off 585,000lb (265,352kg).
Dimensions: Length 174ft 0in (53m); height 55ft 2in (16.8m); wingspan 169ft 9in (51.8m). Cargo compartment 88 x 18 x 12ft (26.8 x 5.5 x 3.8m).
Powerplant: Four Pratt & Whitney F117-PW-100 turbofan engines, each 40,440lb (18,343kg) static thrust.
Performance: Cruise speed at 28,000ft (8,534m) 450 knots (Mach 0.74); service ceiling at cruising speed 45,000ft (13,716m); range at 160,000lb (72,575kg) payload and cruise altitude 28,000ft/8,534m) 2,400nm.
Payload: 102 troops/paratroops; or 36 litter and 54 ambulatory patients and attendants; or 170,900lb (77,519kg) of cargo (18 pallet positions).
Crew: Three (pilot/captain, co-pilot, loadmaster).

The first squadron of this remarkable transport became operational in January 1995 and the Air Force plans to purchase a total of 134, with the last one being delivered in 2005. Of these, 114 will be with active force units, a further 14 with special operations units, and six with the ANG. The C-17 is capable of rapid strategic delivery of troops and all types of cargo to main operating bases or direct to forward bases in the deployment area, but can also perform tactical airdrop missions, when required. The four Pratt & Whitney engines are fitted with thrust reversers to shorten the landing run. Maximum use is made of off-the-shelf equipment, either from commercial sources, or, in the case of the avionics, Air Force-standardized equipment..

There are just three crew: pilot, co-pilot and loadmaster. Cargo is loaded over the rear ramp and the aircraft can carry virtually all the Army's air-transportable equipment. The aircraft is capable of taking off and landing on runways 3,000ft (914m) long and 90ft (27.4m) wide, and even on such a narrow runway it can turn around using a three-point star turn and its backing capability. Some C-17s are modified to fly SOLL-II missions (Special Operations, Low Level - Image Intensifier) in which the flightcrew wear image intensifying goggles enabling them to fly at very low level, and land/take-off, all in total darkness.

▲ **Above** *Despite its size, the C-17 requires a crew of just three people.*

▶ **Right** *Loaded with supplies, C-17s await their turn to take off on an overseas mission.*

C-130 Hercules transport

Manufacturer: Lockheed Martin, USA.

Type: Intratheater airlift.

Weight: Empty 69,300lb (31,434kg); max take-off 135,000lb (61,236kg).

Dimensions: Length 97ft 9in (29.3m); height 38ft 3in (11.4m); wingspan 132ft 7in (39.7m).

Powerplant: Four Rolls-Royce Allison T56-A-15 turboprops; each 4,300shp (3,080kW).

Performance: Max cruising speed 321kt (370mph/595km/h) at 30,000ft (9,144m); range 4,210nm (4,848 miles/7,802km) with max fuel or 1,910nm (2,199 miles/3,539km) with max payload.

Payload: 92 troops or 64 paratroops or 74 litter patients; maximum allowable cabin load 36,000lb.

Crew: Five (two pilots, navigator, flight engineer, loadmaster).

The prototype of this truly great aircraft flew in 1954. Its IOC occurred in 1957, but (in various versions) it remains in large-scale, front-line service with the USAF, Navy and Marine Corps to this day. The current transport model in service with the USAF is the C-130H, which continues to be upgraded, and most have been fitted with the Night Vision Instrumentation System.

The major current upgrade is the C-130 Avionics Modernization Program (C-130X AMP) which will modify approximately 525 in-service aircraft of approximately 13 different sub-types, to establish a common, supportable, cost effective baseline configuration for all C-130 aircraft, with a new avionics suite. The C-130J has a two-crew flight system, four Rolls-Royce-Allison AE-21-00D3 engines, all-composite Dowty propellers, digital avionics and mission computers, enhanced performance, and improved reliability and maintainability. The C-130J-30 is 15ft longer, significantly increasing carrying capacity and range, enabling it to work as a strategic, as well as tactical, transport. Apart from these transports there are many special-purpose versions, including gunships and a wide variety of electronic warfare types.

▲ **Above**   *The C-130 transport aircraft under guard at a US Air Force base. The USAF is still developing new versions with increased payload and performance.*

C-141 StarLifter

Manufacturer: Lockheed Martin, USA.

Type: Strategic cargo and troop transport.

Weight: Max takeoff 323,100lb (146,863kg).

Dimensions: Length 168ft 4in (51m); height 39ft 2in (11.9m); wingspan 160ft 0in (48.7m).

Powerplant: Four Pratt & Whitney TF33-P-7 turbofan engines, each 20,250lb (9,113kg) static thrust.

Performance: Max 500mph (Mach 0.74) at 25,000ft (8,200m); range 2,174nm (2,500 miles /4,023km) on internal fuel.

Payload: 200 troops, or 155 paratroops, or 103 litters plus 14 attendants, or 68,725lb (31,239kg) cargo.

Crew: Five (pilot/captain, copilot, two flight engineers, one loadmaster); for airdrops add navigator.

The C-141 entered service in October 1964 and was immediately involved in the air-bridge to Vietnam. Shortly afterwards, the entire fleet (less four NC-141s) were lengthened by 23.3ft (7.1m), a process which increased fleet capacity by the equivalent of 90 new C-141s. The rebuild also included installing in-flight refueling equipment, which makes the C-141B instantly recognizable by the hump immediately abaft the cockpit. Started in the mid-1970s, the work was completed in June 1982.

The large, uncluttered cargo hold is 10ft 4in wide and 9ft 2in high, with a large rear ramp covered by clamshell doors, which can be opened in flight. There are over 30 different configurations, ranging from rollers for pallets, through smooth floor for vehicles to aft-facing seats for 166 troops and sidewall canvas seats for some 155 fully equipped paratroops. All changes are achieved quickly and economically.

In the aeromedical evacuation role, the Starlifter can carry about 103 litter patients, 113 walking patients or a combination of the two. Some C-141s have been equipped with intra-formation positioning sets that enable a flight of 2 to 36 aircraft to maintain formation regardless of visibility. There are 241 C-141B in the Active Force, 16 in the Air National Guard and 12 in the Reserve Force.

▲ **Above** *C-141s play a key role in establishing an "air bridge" to any area of the world where the US has become militarily involved. This is a C-141B, identified by the "hump" immediately behind the cockpit.*

KC-10A Extender

Manufacturer: Boeing (McDonnell Douglas), USA.

Type: Aerial tanker/transport.

Weight: Empty (tanker) 240,065lb (108,891kg); max takeoff 590,000lb (265,500kg).

Dimensions: Length 181ft 7in (54.4m); height 58ft 1in (17.4m); wingspan: 165ft 5in (50m).

Powerplant: Three General Electric CF6-50C2 turbofans, each 52,500lb (23.3kN) static thrust.

Performance: Max speed (clean) 619mph (Mach 0.83); normal cruising speed at 30,000ft (9,145m) 490kt (564mph/908km/h); ceiling 42,000ft (12,727m); range with cargo 3,800nm (4,400 miles/7,080km); without cargo 10,000nm (11,500 miles/18,500km).

Payload: Max cargo payload 170,000lb (76,560kg); max fuel load 356,000lb (160,200kg).

Crew: Four (aircraft commander, pilot, flight engineer, boom operator).

Based on the DC-10 airliner, the KC-10A has three additional tanks under the cargo floor, giving a total fuel capacity of 356,000lb (160,200kg). Inflight transfer of fuel is achieved either by the USAF's boom system, or by a hose-and-drogue centerline system, as used by US Navy and Marine Corps aircraft and virtually all foreign air forces. The KC-10A can conduct night air refueling operations, and can itself be air-refueled by another tanker.

The KC-l0A has a large cargo door and powered rollers and winches to permit moving heavy loads, enabling it to be used as a transport, for 27 pallets or a mixed load of 17 pallets and 75 passengers. The normal crew is four, but additional seats and bunks can be installed for extra crew members. There are 59 KC-10s in service, all with active units of the US Air Force.

▼ **Below** *Airborne tankers such as this KC-10, have a very unglamorous mission but play a vital role as "force multipliers," extending the range and endurance of any aircraft, from fighters to this C-141 transport.*

KC-135R Stratotanker

Manufacturer: Boeing, USA.

Type: Aerial tanker/transport.

Weight: Empty 106,306lb (48,220kg); max takeoff 322,500lb (146,285kg).

Dimensions: Length 136ft 4in (415m); height 41.7ft (12.7m); wingspan 130.8ft (39.9m).

Powerplant: Four CFM International CFM-56 turbofan engines, each 21,634lb (9,813kg) static thrust.

Performance: Speed 530mph at 30,000ft (9,144m); ceiling: 50,000ft (15,240m); range 1,500 miles (2,419km) with 150,000lb (68,039kg) of transfer fuel; ferry mission, up to 11,015 miles (17,766km).

Payload: Max transferable fuel 200,000lb (90,719kg); max cargo capability 83,000lb (37,648kg); 37 passengers.

Crew: Four (pilot, co-pilot, navigator, boom operator).

In the 1980s Boeing re-engined 410 KC-135As with CFM-56 turbofans, which are more powerful, as well as quieter and more economical. Designated KC-135R, this aircraft can offload 50 percent more fuel, is 25 percent more fuel efficient, and costs 25 percent less to operate than the KC-135A. The KC-135R also has an on-board auxiliary power unit (APU) enabling it to operate autonomously away from main bases.

The present inventory totals 545 tankers, of which 253 are with the active force (all KC-135R), while the Air National Guard and Air Force Reserve operate 292, a mix of KC-135Rs and KC-135Es. Originally, the KC-135 was capable of refueling only by using the flying boom system, but it can now also refuel using the probe-and-drogue method.

▲ **Above**   *KC-135 Stratotanker refuels an E-4 airborne command post using the USAF's "flying boom" system, which is controlled by an operator in a special cabin on the underside of the tanker aircraft.*

IRAQI CW/BW DELIVERY SYSTEMS

As described elsewhere in this book, the Iraqis continue to develop their BW/CW capability and part of this evil program includes the means of delivering such agents. The Iraqis have carried out delivery tests using aircraft, and two methods at least have been tested: using a spray system converted from an agricultural crop sprayer, and drop

▶ **Left**   *An Iraqi Mirage F1 shown spraying a simulated BW agent from specially adapted drop tanks in a January 1991 trial.*

tanks. Early trials involved a converted MiG-21 and later trials have taken place using a Mirage F1. The most likely platform, however, is the Aero L-29 Delfin.

This is a Czech-built, two-seat trainer, of which a number have been converted into unmanned aerial vehicles (UAVs) whose maximum weight is 7,800lb. Length is 35ft 5in, height 10ft 3in and wingspan 33ft 9in. It is powered by a turbojet with 1,962lb static thrust; top speed is a little over 400mph at sea level, cruise is 285mph, service ceiling is 36,000ft and range is about 400 miles.

US forces would find an incoming L-29 carrying drop tanks filled with chemical or biological agents to be a relatively slow-moving target, capable of making only limited maneuvers, and therefore easy to hit. But the problem for the defense will be how to destroy it without releasing its payload over friendly troops or population either in the attack or in the subsequent crash.

IRAQI AIR DEFENSE COMMAND

It will be clear from the foregoing description of the shortage of numbers, elderly designs and poor servicing of equipment of the Iraqi Air Force that it stands little chance of defending the country against air attacks by the United States and its allies. Of possibly greater significance is the ground-based Iraqi Air Defense Command, which comes under Air Force command.

The Israeli attack on the Iraqi nuclear reactor at Osirak in 1981 led to the establishment of a Soviet pattern networked, multi-layered, resilient, wide-area air defense system, using a mix of fighters, guns and missiles. The main concentrations were around high-value strategic and industrial facilities in and around Baghdad, with a nationwide command and control system, based on an Air Defense Operations Center (ADOC) in Baghdad and four subordinate Sector Operations Centers (SOC), each controlling a specific geographic area. Virtually all these command centers were in deep-buried bunkers and were linked to each other and to other national headquarters, primarily by microwave telecommunications systems.

Following the 1991 Gulf War debacle, Saddam gave top priority to rebuilding the air defense system, and while it is not as effective as in mid-1990, the 2003 system is potentially reasonably effective. By circumventing UN sanctions, the Iraqis have purchased equipment from wherever they can find it in the global market place, much of it not the most technologically advanced. A fringe benefit for the Iraqis,

▲ **Above** *The Iraqi Air Defense Command uses Russian-supplied ZSU-23-4 AA guns developed some forty years ago. American ECM aircraft should have little trouble jamming the radar.*

▲ **Above** *ECM flares launched by this F/A-18 fighter (and many other US warplanes) are effective in confusing and thwarting surface-to-air missiles.*

System	Origin	Altitude	Mobility	TOTALS
SA-7	USSR	14,000ft		
SA-14 Gremlin	USSR	20,000ft	Man- portable	1,500
SA-16 Gimlet	USSR	15,000ft		
SA-2 Guideline	USSR	90,000ft	Towed launchers	125
Hawk	USA	66,000ft		See note
SA-3 Goa	USSR	40,000ft		100
SA-8 Gecko	USSR	40,000ft	Wheeled launcher	Ca. 80
SA-9/-13	USSR	11,500ft		125
Crotale	France	28,000ft		Some
SA-6 Gainful	USSR	60,000ft	Tracked launcher	Ca. 50
Roland	France	19,000ft		Some
Aspide	Italy	20,000ft	Unknown	Some

Note: A complete US-built Hawk battery was removed from Kuwait by the Iraqis during the occupation and has never been accounted for.

Iraqi surface-to-air-missile launchers

System	Caliber	Altitude (max)*	Firing rate	Mobility	TOTALS
ZSU-23-4	23mm	17,000ft	800rpm	SP – tracks	
M-1939	37mm	20,000ft	80rpm	Towed – wheels	
ZSU-57-2	57mm	20,000ft	140rpm	SP – tracks	approx
KS-18 (M-1944)	85mm	40,000ft?	10-15rpm	Towed – wheels	6,000
KS-19M2 (M-1949)	100mm	47,000ft	15-20 rpm	Towed – wheels	
KS-30 (M-1955)	130mm	72,000ft	10-12 rpm	Towed – wheels	

* These are "book" figures. In practice, the effective ceiling will be somewhat less and, if deprived of radar control by US ECM and firing under visual control, the effective ceiling will be at least halved.

Iraqi air defense gun systems

however, is that this has added to the uncertainty of US and Coalition planners and flyers, since instead of being faced by a well-understood Soviet system they now have to overcome a system made up of many disparate elements, comprising a mixture of the old Soviet system, some European elements and a number of Far Eastern, mainly Chinese, sub-systems. Another improvement for the Iraqis is that, having discovered in 1991 that the microwave links, despite their narrow beams, could be detected by US electronic warfare systems, and then either monitored, jammed, or destroyed, many of these links have been replaced by fiberglass cables, the work being done by Chinese contractors.

Iraq's Air Defense Command is currently estimated to have a strength of some 17,000 troops and its main items of equipment are shown in the accompanying tables.

Air Defense Command – Special Republican Guard (SRG)

A uniquely Iraqi element is the Special Republican Guard Air Defense Group which consists of ten batteries, each tasked with the protection of specific targets of significance to Saddam Hussein. These protected sites include the Baghdad international airport and several others in the city, as well as Saddam's palaces and his birthplace. There is also a mobile battery to protect motorcades.

THE LAND CAMPAIGN

Today, the Iraqi armed forces once again face a land battle which will undoubtedly be fought on several fronts, but which will not end this time until the last vestige of Saddam Hussein's evil regime has been swept away, and his apparatus of torture and repression totally dismantled.

On the land, as in the air, Saddam Hussein is facing the "mother of all defeats." He may well have 2,000 main battle tanks, 3,000 armored personnel carriers, and 2,000 artillery pieces, but they are not at all well maintained. They and his 300,000 poorly equipped troops will be subjected to an aerial barrage by day and by night that will mightily damage if not destroy his command and control and communication systems, completely annihilate any semblance of air support, cause catastrophe to his resupply resources, and result in untold numbers of casualties who will not be able to be treated properly because of the continuing onslaught.

When the American ground attack starts, some 2,500 high-speed, heavily armed and well-protected main battle tanks and armored fighting vehicles, plus 400-odd self-propelled guns and other artillery pieces, will thrust into action from across the Kuwaiti border and other regions, supported by at least 300 attack helicopters. All of this equipment will be operated by rigorously trained soldiers and Marines itching to get into battle. It will be of the best quality and maintained to the highest standards – and backed by a highly efficient, capable and resilient communications and logistics system.

The endgame, and the gameplan, may be different from the events of twelve years ago, but it is difficult to see a different result than when the much-vaunted Iraqi Army was totally overwhelmed, outgeneraled, outmaneuvered and outfought by Coalition forces under United States' leadership in Operation Desert Storm. Then, the land campaign lasted just 100 hours. Indeed, it was only because the United States decided that its war aims had been achieved by recapturing Kuwait that Iraq was not comprehensively overrun and its leadership deposed and put on trial for crimes against humanity.

In the coming campaign the commander-in-chief of the United States' Central Command (CENTCOM) is once again assured of air supremacy and command of the seas – and especially of the Gulf. But it is what happens on land that will decide the issue. During Desert Storm the Coalition land force was made up of many disparate elements, but this time there are likely to be just a very few. Even so, the United States Army and Marines are perfectly capable of assembling overwhelming force and deploying it rapidly to the Gulf.

Saddam Hussein faces some major challenges. His land forces are already weak and ill-prepared, but it seems very probable that he will have to split them into three groups, one each to counter the threatened invasions from the north and the south, while the third will have to be

◁ **Left** *Cornerstone of the land battle, a US Army M1 tank fires at Iraqi targets in the 1991 Gulf War.*

retained to maintain control over internal dissidents, some of whom are bound to seize this opportunity for a popular uprising.

Long-serving and vicious dictators such as Saddam are always surrounded by "yes-men" who scrupulously avoid bringing bad news to their ruler. But even the Iraqi dictator is completely out of touch with reality if he does not realize that his forces are weak and their equipment is out-dated, short of spares and badly maintained.

Clearly, Operation Desert Storm provides many indicators for an attack twelve years later. The 1991 land battle started at 8pm on Sunday 24 February. Allied units rolled across the border into Iraq and Kuwait from Saudi Arabia to the south after 38 days and nights of bombing of targets across the length and breadth of Iraq.

Coalition commander General H. Norman ("Stormin' Norman") Schwarzkopf had, like many generations of military officers, been fascinated by the battle of Cannae which took place in the year 216BC. Then, an outnumbered Carthaginian force under the command of Hannibal surrounded and destroyed a massive Roman army. For the

▲ **Above** *Another cornerstone – an M16A2-armed infantryman of the US Army.*

trapped legions, this encirclement and destruction produced a casualty rate to rival that of the atomic bombs over Hiroshima or Nagasaki two

▲ **Above** *Coalition commander-in-chief in the Gulf War, General Norman Schwarzkopf's victory was one of the greatest and most comprehensive military triumphs of the 20th century.*

millennia later. Ever since, to wise commanders Cannae has represented a specter of defeat, a warning that even the biggest and most combat-seasoned army could be dragged down to destruction. In February 1991 Schwarzkopf – also known to his men as "The Bear" – was about to emulate the Carthaginian military leader he had for so long admired.

With their air force effectively knocked out in the first days of the air war, the Iraqis had almost no reconnaissance information. The only imagery they could gather was that broadcast from the three US NOA weather satellites. Flying in polar orbit, these provided low-resolution imagery of the Gulf six times a day. Taken in visible light and IR wavelengths, such images were too small in scale to show military targets, only the degree of cloud cover over Allied bases and operational areas. As a result, the Iraqi general staff probably knew little more about the Allied deployment against them than what they – or anybody else around the world – could obtain by watching CNN's TV news programs.

Effectively blinded, the Iraqis had to rely on cross-border raids and their limited SIGINT (signals intelligence) capability when trying to build up a picture of the Allied formations moving into place along the border in mid-February. As a result, they became the target of a massive deception operation in which recorded radio traffic was transmitted from areas south of Kuwait vacated by Allied units sent to join the main force building up on the left flank.

With its air defenses stripped away by the bombing campaign, the Iraqi Army had been opened up to round-the-clock air attack. Unable to move without exposing themselves to bombardment, Iraq's thousands of main battle tanks and artillery pieces had been destroyed in large numbers, and their resupply system brought to a shuddering halt.

As a result, when the main Allied ground attack was unleashed, American, British And French tanks and APCs sliced through the defenses at a speed that surprised even the most optimistic observers. Vehicle top speeds are usually "book" figures, attainable only in test runs in the best conditions. However, the new generation powerplant and suspension systems of the Western AFVs, especially that of the M1A1 Abrams tank and the Bradley infantry fighting vehicle, made for real operational gains in speed and mobility. The fast-moving, freewheeling tactics of the Allied armored forces came as a devastating shock to an Iraqi Army used to dealing with massed frontal assaults by ill-trained and slow-moving Iranian infantry.

The French "Daguet" 6th Light Division was trained and equipped to fight in exactly this kind of terrain. Operating with elements of the US 82nd Airborne Division, it advanced over 60 miles into Iraq within hours to secure the western flanks of the land operation. Slightly to the east, AirLand battle tactics were epitomized by the US 101st Airborne Division – the pioneers of the "Air

◀ **Left** *The fast and well-armed M1 Abrams performed remarkably well during Desert Storm in 1991, earning a fully justified reputation as a great tank, and the Iraqis still have nothing to compare.*

▼ **Below** *Many Iraqi armored units are equipped with the obsolete Soviet T-54s and T-55s, whose ammunition cannot penetrate an M1 hull, and whose own hull is penetrated with ease by the M1's 120mm rounds.*

▲ **Above** *Despite ever-increasing numbers of M2 Bradley Infantry Fighting Vehicles (IFVs), there are still many of the solid and reliable M113 to be found serving throughout the US Army.*

◄ **Left** *The Russian-supplied T-72 is found only in Iraqi Republican Guard armored units.*

Cav" role. The biggest helicopter lift in history established a massive logistics and fire base some 60 miles into Iraq, from which airmobile units leapt forward again to seize river crossings on the Euphrates, in conjunction with the US 24th Mechanized Division.

Meanwhile, heavy units of the US lst Armored, 3rd Armored, 1st Infantry, lst Cavalry and British 1st Armoured Divisions poured through the Iraqi border defenses near the west edge of the Kuwait-Saudi Arabia border, swinging round to the east to destroy the Republican Guard and cut off the Iraqi Army in Kuwait. Egyptian, Saudi and Kuwaiti forces pushed into Kuwait itself, supported by the US 1st and 2nd Marine Divisions.

What rapidly became apparent was the startling disparity in effectiveness between Iraqi and Coalition forces. Even allowing for the chaos in their command and control system, the disruption to their supplies and the morale effects of 38 days of bombing, the Iraqi Army achieved remarkably little. The performance of elderly T-55 and T-62 tanks against M-1Als and British Challengers was perhaps no surprise, but not even the modern T-72 was able to cause any tank casualties to the Allies. While Iraq's artillery equipment could have been expected to equal or even outperform that of the Coalition, without air cover and lacking in target acquisition the guns and their ammunition supply system were rapidly destroyed.

IRAQI GROUND FORCES ORGANIZATION

The organization of the Iraqi ground forces is appreciably different from that of the United States or its allies. In part this is due to following the pattern taught them by the Soviet instructors who helped organize and equip the Iraqi Army for many years. But it is also due to the existence of organizations such as the Republican Guard and *Fedayeen Saddam* which have no parallels in Western armed forces.

Army

The Iraqi Army is currently some 375,000 strong. Of these, at least a third are reservists, and their mobilization would be easy for Western intelligence to detect. The

Divisions		Composition				
Type	Number in 2002	Armored Brigade	Mechanized Brigade	Infantry Brigade	Tank Battalion	Artillery Battalion
Armored	3	2	1			4
Mechanized	3	1	2			4
Infantry	11			2	1	4

Iraqi Army – late 2002

Army is beset by problems, resulting from ethnic and religious tensions (Kurds and Shias cannot be officers), factionalism (even among the Sunni majority), and its history of defeats. In addition, the UN sanctions have not only prevented the Army from acquiring new equipment but have also ensured that most of the spares needed to keep its existing equipment serviceable have failed to get through.

To add to the problems besetting the Army there are at least four other organizations with military and quasi-military roles – Republican Guard, Special Republican Guard, Brigade 999 and the *Fedayeen Saddam* – and which generally receive better equipment, pay and privileges than those enjoyed by the Army proper.

The Army's operational command level is at corps, each of which exercises control over a designated geographical area, within which it is responsible for all ground combat activities, together with administrative and logistical support of the forces under command. There are currently seven such corps. Each is allocated a number of divisions, usually three or four, and also exercises direct command over its "corps assets" such as artillery and helicopters. Corps headquarters normally operate from above-ground buildings, but have underground bunkers for wartime use and can also deploy a mobile, field command post.

At the start of the Gulf War in 1991 the Iraqi Army had some 7 armored and mechanized divisions and 20 infantry divisions. Following the heavy losses in the war and the subsequent reorganization and rebuilding, it is now only about 17 divisions strong. At the end of 2002, these were organized into three armored divisions, three mechanized divisions, and 11 infantry divisions.

> **"Iraqi divisions should not be compared to a US division on a one-for-one basis..."**

Like most armies, Iraqi's Army depends upon reservists to complete its order of battle prior to the outbreak of war, and thus many of these formations will be considerably undermanned in peace. It is particularly important to note that these Iraqi divisions should not be compared to a US division on a one-for-one basis, since American divisions are much larger, much better equipped, and with infinitely greater standards of command, control, communications, maintenance and reliability.

The rebuilding process has not been easy, partly because of UN sanctions, but also because of the need to maintain the repressive and unpopular regime by conducting continuing active operations against the Shi'ite minority in the south and the Kurds in the north. There has also been the need to protect the regime against challenges from the civil population in the Sunni areas, and the whole process has been further complicated by a series of attempted coups led by senior military officers, for whom the price of failure has been a painful death.

The Republican Guard

Many dictatorial regimes find it necessary to raise an ideologically reliable military force, as, for example, Hitler did with the German *Waffen-SS*. In the Iraqi case, this is the Republican Guard, which originated as a relatively small force intended only to protect Saddam's numerous palaces. However, when the regular Army performed particularly badly during the Iran-Iraq war, the guard raised an armored brigade whose performance in battle so impressed Saddam that he made it permanent and ordered that more such units be formed. Despite its reputation, the Republican Guard did not do well during the Gulf War, and lost a great deal of men and equipment, particularly to air attack.

Officers and men of the Republican Guard are given higher pay, generous allowances, special privileges and the best military equipment available. Despite all this, it is proving impossible to find sufficient men to pass the stringent intake tests. As a result, the Republican Guard is currently estimated to be only some 70,000 strong (against about 150,000 in 1991), although it is still organized into the same six divisions – three armored, one mechanized and two infantry – as it was twelve years ago.

There have been recent reports, however, that parts, at least, of the Republican Guard have been reorganized into small combat groups, perhaps of company size, which are intended to conduct independent guerrilla operations in the rear areas of an advancing army. Such groups would wear civilian clothing and have detailed local knowledge and would almost certainly making use of prepositioned weapons caches. Then, depending on their skill and determination, they could make life difficult – at least in the short term – for American and Allied forces.

Special Republican Guard

To overcome the increasing problem of insuring the political reliability of the Republican Guard, Saddam has formed the Special Republican Guard (in effect, an elite within an elite) which is some 15,000 strong, with a further 10,000 reservists, who are organized into four "Special Republican Guard brigades."

Fedayeen Saddam

In 1995 Saddam's son, Uday, founded a new paramilitary force known as the *Fedayeen Saddam* (*fedayeen* = men of sacrifice). Despite the fact that the unit bore his father's name, Uday appears to have intended to develop a powerful force answerable only to himself. The strength built up rapidly and in March 1996 Uday masterminded the compulsory transfer of some sophisticated military equipment from the Republican Guard to his *Fedayeen Saddam*. This time, however, he had overstepped the mark as he had failed to obtain his father's prior approval, and when this came to light in September 1996 he was summarily removed from his post. Curiously, at least to outside observers, the *Fedayeen Saddam* was neither disbanded nor placed under either the Army or the Republican Guard, but remains in existence, albeit now under command of another of Saddam's sons, Qu'say.

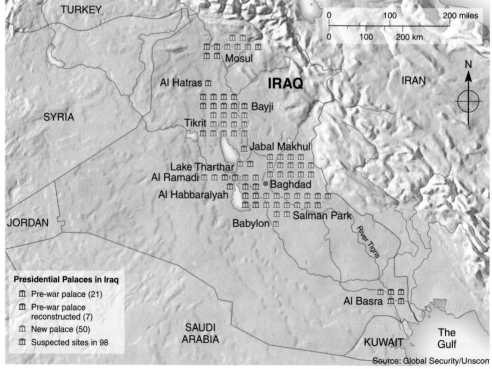

▲ **Above** *Saddam's presidential palaces are immensely grand and very costly, and why he should require so many is a complete mystery; it seems possible that they serve a sinister purpose, as yet unknown.*

The strength of the *Fedayeen* is estimated at 35,000-40,000. Its members are recruited from areas and tribes known to be loyal to Saddam Hussein. Their tasks include operations against Iraqi dissidents, particularly in the south, as well as spreading a reign of terror in the main cities, but it has also been suggested that they are being trained to hijack airliners. It seems possible, therefore, that they may be being prepared for terrorist attacks – possibly suicidal – along the lines of the Palestinian fedayeen.

Special Forces

The term "special forces" is used differently for the Iraqi armed forces than it is for Western forces. Iraq's "special forces" are more akin to specially selected and trained light infantry, unlike American, British or French special forces whose primary missions are strategic. Thus, the Iraqi Army includes two Special Forces Brigades, but their normal missions are tactical assaults in support of corps or divisional missions and include parachute or heliborne assaults in wartime, or anti-subversion missions in peacetime, almost all of them in support of conventional forces.

UNITED STATES GROUND FORCE ORGANIZATION

The land battle will be commanded by a US Army Corps headquarters, located within the war zone. There is no standard organization for such a Corps, which will be given the assets it needs, with individual components being added or removed as the campaign progresses. However, it is probable that the Corps will comprise six armored divisions, five of which will be US and one British. These armored divisions are the basic maneuver formations at the tactical level and perform the major tactical operations for the corps. They contain their own maneuver, combat support and logistic units, but also gain support from the Corps units. These Corps units will include most, if not all, of the following:

- **Armored Cavalry Regiment** (ACR), which conducts reconnaissance, security, and economy of force operations.
- **Aviation Brigade**, whose primary assets are three AH-64 battalions and an aviation group.
- **Corps Artillery**, which includes all those field artillery cannon, guided missile, and multiple rocket launcher battalions not organic to the maneuver divisions.

▲ **Above**   *US Special Operations Forces (as well as those of Israel, and perhaps the UK) reportedly began observation and other operations deep in Iraq in mid-2002; their experiences in dealing with the terrain, climate and people will serve them well.*

TYPE	EQUIPMENT	QUANTITY HELD 2002	PROVIDER	NUMBER SUPPLIED	DATE SUPPLIED	REMARKS
MBT	T-55	2,200	USSR	700	1960s-70s	
	T-62		USSR	>400	1970s	
	PRC Type 59		PRC	1,500	1960s-70s	
	T-72		USSR	400	1980s	
RECCE	BRDM-2,	400	USSR	>300		4 x 4 armd C
	AML-60		France	70	1970s	4 x 4 Armd C
	EE-9 Cascavel		Brazil	750	1970s	6 x 6 armd C
	EE-3 Jararaca		Brazil	300	1980s	4 x 4 armd C
AIFV	BMP-1/-2	900	USSR	1000	1970s/80s	
APC	BTR-50/-60/152	2,400	USSR	>1000		8 x 8 wheeled
	OT-62/-64		Czecho-slovakia	>200	1960s	Version of BTR-50P. Prodn ended 1971
	MTLB		USSR	<100	1960s	
	YW-701		PRC	<100		Tracked comd vehicle
	M-113A1 /A2			<50		Captured from Iran
	EE-11 Urutu		Brazil	500	1980s	
Towed Arty	105mm M-56	1,900	Italy			Pack/howitzer
	122mm D-74		USSR			In prodn 1950s-60s
	122mm D-30		USSR			In prodn 1960s-70s
	122mm M-1938 (M- 30)		USSR			In prodn 1940s-50s
	130mm M46		USSR			In prodn 1950s-60s
	130mm Type 59-1		PRC			In prodn 1960s-80s
	155mm G-5		RSA	A few		Some reached Iraq
	155mm GHN-45		Austria			Bull design. Ammo from Belgium
	155mm M-114		USA	A few		Captured from Iran
SP ARTY	122mm 2S1	150	USSR		1970s-80s	
	152mm2S3		USSR		1970s-80s	
	155mm M109A1/A2		USA			Captured from Iran
	155mm AUF-1 (GCT)		France	85	1970s-80s	Delivered direct

Notes:
1. All quantities are estimates.
2. 50 percent of all equipment lacks spares and overall serviceability is poor.
3. The Iraqis have also mounted the 160mm mortar on the T-55 tank chassis.

TYPE	EQUIPMENT	QUANTITY HELD 2002	PROVIDER	NUMBER SUPPLIED	DATE SUPPLIED	REMARKS
MRL	BM-21	200	USSR			122mm
	ASTROS II		Brazil			70mm
	BM-13/46		USSR			132mm
	Ababeel		Iraq			400mm rocket
MOR	5lmm	>1,500	USSR			
	120mm		USSR			
	160mm		USSR			
	M-1943 240mm		USSR			
Rockets	up to 50 FROG	<50	USSR			On 8 x 8 wheeled Zil launchers
Missiles	Scud launchers (ca27 missiles)	6	USSR			On 8 x 8 MAZ wheeled launchers
RCL	73mm SPG-9	?	USSR			
	82mm B-10		USSR			
	107mm B-11		USSR			
ATk Guns	85mm		USSR			Probably Towed
	Soviet D-48	100m.		USSR		Probably Soviet T-12
Attack	Bo-105	Ca. 100	Germany			AS-11 /HOT
Helicopters	Mi-24		USSR	ca. 40	1980s	Including -D, -E, -F
	SA-316		France			Alouette
	SA-321		France	16	1977	Frelon
	SA-342		? France			Gazelle
Transport	Mi-6	<300	USSR	Few		NATO = Hook
helicopters	AS-61		Italy	6	1980s	SH-3D derivative
	Bell 214 ST		USA	45	1985-90	Sold to Iraq for civil use
	Mi-8/-17		USSR	ca. 100	1970s-80s	NATO = Hip
	SA-330		France	22	1980s	Puma
	AB-212		Italy	10	1983-89	Ordered but may not have been delivered
	BK-117		Germany	16	1985-89	Intended for SAR but have military value
	Hughes 300/500		USA			Civil models impressed by military
Infantry	7.62mm PK/RPK		USSR	>200,000		
MGs	Rifle7.62mm AK-47		USSR	>200,000		
	7.62mm SVD		USSR	<1,000		Sniper rifle

- **Engineer Brigade**, controlling engineer units which are not organic to maneuver divisions to provide mobility, countermobility, and survivability, topographic engineering, and general engineering support to the Corps. The brigade contains combat engineer battalions, and additional separate engineer companies, bridging and topographic companies, as required by the operations.

- **Air Defense Artillery (ADA) Brigade**, providing an area defense system.

- **Signal Brigade**, which installs, operates and maintains voice and data communications within and between the Corps command and control facilities, as well as an extensive area network that connects all elements of the Corps.

- **Chemical Brigade**, which commands, controls, and coordinates the chemical warfare (CW) operations of attached

▲ **Above** *The Iraqis have no better answer now than they did in 1991 to the very dangerous AH-64 which can attack troop concentrations and heavy armor by day or by night.*

▶ **Right** *The US and her allies have long been equipped for the Iraqis' greatest battlefield threat – BW/CW agents.*

	Troops	Tanks (all M1)	IFV/CFV (all M2/M3)	AH-64	SP artillery	Towed artillery	MLRS
Armored Division	16,000	348	216	44	72	0	9
Armored Division	16,000	348	216	44	72	0	9
Mechanized Division	14,000	290	270	44	72	0	9
Mechanized Division	14,000	290	270	44	72	0	9
Air Assault	12,000	0	0	84	0	72	0
Corps Troops	50,000	100	100	44	72	0	18
Others	128,000						
TOTAL	250,000	1376	1072	304	360	72	54

Notes:
1. These figures are estimates based on plans announced in 2002 to field a US Army Corps headquarters and five divisions (unspecified), with an initial personnel complement of 250,000 troops.
2. Equipment figures do not include war reserve stocks which may be either ashore or afloat but not committed.
3. "Others" includes USN, USMC, USAF, CG, logistics (other than Corps troops), etc.
4. In the 1991 Gulf War, there were 1,772 tanks ashore (with 528 in reserve), 189 MLRS launchers and 274 AH-64 attack helicopters.

Estimated US ground forces and major equipment in theater at outbreak of Gulf War 2003

chemical units. The brigade provides smoke generator, NBC reconnaissance, and NBC decontamination support in the Corps area.
- **Military Intelligence (MI) Brigade**.
- **Psychological operations (PSYOP) Support Battalion**, which conducts tactical PSYOP and counterpropaganda .
- **Civil Affairs Brigade**.
- **Military Police (MP) Brigade**, consisting of up to 6 MP battalions and providing battlefield traffic control, area security, enemy prisoner-of-war and civilian internee operations, and law-and-order support to the Corps. It conducts reconnaissance and surveillance to ensure security of main supply routes, and area reconnaissance of other key areas in the Corps rear.
- **Finance Group**, which commands, controls, and coordinates the finance operations of all finance battalions in the Corps. It provides administrative and logistical support to assigned finance battalions.
- **Personnel Group**, whose primary responsibility is to operate the Corps Personnel Management Center formed from the AG and personnel operations.
- **Corps Support Command (COSCOM)**, which is the principal logistic organization in the Corps, providing supply, field services, transportation, maintenance, and combat health support to all units in the Corps area.

OPERATIONAL DISPARITIES

Iraq will suffer from great disparities in a number of significant areas during the land combat phase of the next war. With regard to tanks, the United States has a homogenous force of M1s, which are well-armed, well-protected, fast, agile and carefully controlled to ensure that they act in a concerted manner. Similarly, the infantry is mounted in M2 Bradleys, while the artillery is all self-propelled, and both are well able to keep up with the tanks. There is also a host of armed helicopters, able to operate deep inside hostile territory, as well as transport helicopters, which can move troops around the battlefield or provide resupply.

Against this, while the Iraqis may have numerical superiority in-theater in some cases, they suffer from a severe qualitative disadvantage in all aspects, since they operate numbers of models of outdated equipment, with poorer performance, and with far less reliability. What may not be so readily apparent, however, are some other disadvantages. The Iraqis have extremely limited surveillance and reconnaissance capabilities, with just a very few UAVs, and even the very small number reconnaissance aircraft are unlikely to survive while overflying US Army or Marine Corps positions.

The United States will have more than sufficient information

Country/Region	Total troops	Permanent US facilities	Prepositioned (prepo) stocks	Remarks
BAHRAIN	4,200	HQ 5th Fleet 1 airbase	Yes	
DJIBOUTI	80+ SOF	No	?	Known also to be op base for UAV
KUWAIT	9,000	1 brigade HQ 2 army bases 1 airbase 2 Patriot batteries	2 x armored brigade	Usually 1 CONUS-based armored brigade on exercise
OMAN	2,400	Yes	?	
QATAR	4,000	1 x airbase	1 x armored brigade	Fwd HQ CENTCOM fm Nov 02 (600 people)
SAUDI ARABIA*	6,000	Several bases 1 Patriot battery	Yes	HQ facilities at Prince Sultan airbase
TURKEY	2,000	NATO HQ	Yes	Most at Incirlik**
UNITED ARAB EMIRATES	500		No	
AT SEA	20,000	1 x CVBG in Gulf 1 x CVBG in Indian Ocean		

* Saudi Arabia has stated opposition to a U.S. invasion of Iraq, but position is softening.
** Warplanes patrolling Iraq's northern no-fly zone are based here.

US military forces normally stationed in Gulf area in late 2002 (does not include major reinforcements for operations in Iraq)

from its mix of satellites, reconnaissance aircraft, helicopters, UAVs and electronic warfare systems, while Iraqi commanders will be almost completely in the dark, as, indeed, they were during the Gulf War.

Similarly, in the sphere of command, control and communications, the United States has a wealth of efficient and resilient systems to ensure that its forces act in a coordinated and properly controlled manner, with each element cooperating with every other element. Thus, its commanders will be able to deploy and control its assets to ensure maximum combat effectiveness.

On the Iraqi side the communications systems will be subjected to strong electronic attack by US electronic warfare systems, leaving superior command echelons deprived of information passing up the command chain, while the subordinate units will be without orders or direction coming down from above.

Finally in this list of operational disparities is the question of resupply. The United States has a comprehensive system which will insure that units are constantly resupplied with whatever replacement manpower, equipment, ammunition, spare parts, food or fuel they need. Furthermore, the Iraqis will be so outnumbered in the air that they will be unable to disrupt the US system, except possibly by the occasional Scud attack. Even if this did occur, the US supply system will simply adopt alternative routes or put in extra men and equipment, so that the front-line units will probably never know that there was a problem. Against this, the Iraqis have a system which has few replenishment stocks to deliver in the first place, and which is totally dependent upon land transport, which will be disrupted on a regular basis, if not totally destroyed, by US air interdiction.

ARMORED WARFARE

As was so conclusively demonstrated in the 1991 Gulf War, the key to modern land campaigns is the mobile battle in which forces of all arms (i.e., tanks, infantry, artillery and aviation)

▲ **Above** *SOF troops (probably SEALs) of Task Force K-BAR, tough and specially trained for surveillance and direct action, including attacks on camps suspected of containing al-Qaeda or other terrorist suspects.*

▲ **Above** *One of the US Army's most powerful assets in the land battle is the MLRS, which brings devastating firepower to bear, although its firing rate is so high that it imposes a significant load on the logistic system.*

▲ **Above** *Base protection is highly important to US forces: the USAF FPAS (Force Protection Airborne System), already deployed in the Gulf, is designed to extend the surveillance range of sentries at facilities with long perimeters, such as air bases.*

▲ **Above** *USMC LAVs in desert terrain. The Marine Corps did not play as full a part in Desert Storm as it wished and will be pressing hard for a much higher profile contribution to the war against Iraq in 2003.*

deploy across the battlefield in order to outmaneuver, destroy and outfight the enemy. At the outbreak of the Gulf War in 1991 the Iraqi Army operated some 5,500 MBTs, of which about 4,500 were in the south and committed during the operations against the Coalition. This was one of the largest tank fleets in the world at that time, and included many thousands provided by the USSR and China, plus a number of US and British types captured from the enemy during the 1980-88 Iran-Iraq War. During the Gulf War, however, the Iraqi armored forces performed very poorly, and while a few units put up a relatively spirited resistance, in general they were comprehensively outmaneuvered and outfought, and lost at least half their tanks.

In 2003, the Iraqi tank fleet is something over 2,000 strong, although it should be noted that, in common, with its other equipment, the Army is struggling to keep the tanks on the road, let alone improve their performance or capabilities. Iraq is known to have a tank repair capability but it is severely limited by a lack of foreign-supplied spares, although it has been reported that a factory has been set up to manufacture some spares for the T-72.

An additional problem has been that very few of the tanks damaged during the Gulf War were recovered by the Army; instead, they were lost to and disposed of by the Coalition forces. It should also be noted that the armored forces shares with the artillery the problem of having old

ammunition, which will almost certainly have degraded in performance and accuracy due to the many years it has spent in storage. In all areas performance will be affected by the lack of spare parts and poor maintenance.

There are four main types of tank in Iraqi service, three of which were supplied by the USSR – T-55, T-62 and T-72. The fourth, the T-59, was developed and built in China, albeit having been based originally on the Soviet T-54. The tanks that Iraq captured during the war with Iran, and which may still be in storage could include US M48s and M60s, as well as British Chieftains. It is likely, however, that these are unusable, due either to lack of spare parts or to lack of ammunition, although efforts may have been made to transfer some of the equipment to other tanks.

The poor quality of the Iraqi armored forces might have been offset by an effective array of anti-tank weapons. But, once again, this is not the case.

Iraqi anti-tank defenses consist of a mix of very elderly Soviet anti-tank guns, including the 85mm D-48 and 100mm T-12, and recoilless rocket launchers (RCL). The anti-tank guided missiles (ATGM) are a mix of Russian types (AT-3 Spigot and AT-3 Sagger), and the French-supplied SS-11, Milan and HOT. All of these employ very antiquated technology and do not pose a significant threat to modern tanks such as the M1 Abrams, although they might be effective against APCs such as the M113. They would certainly be effective against soft-skinned trucks, provided they could get within range, but these are scarcely rewarding targets for an anti-tank weapon.

▲ **Above** *In 1991-92, US Marines gained valuable experience in Afghanistan for the next Gulf War in Iraq; these men are weighed down with supplies and ammunition for three days, but are still able to fight and destroy the enemy.*

▲ **Above** *It is known that during its war with Iran, Iraq captured a great deal of material including tanks, such as M48s, like those seen here. If the Iraqis have been able to find spares, such tanks may be returned to service.*

T-55 Main Battle Tank

Country of origin: Russia.

Crew: 4.

Armament: One 100mm gun; one SGMT 7.62mm co-axial machine gun, two SGMT 7.62mm anti-aircraft machine guns.

Armor: 150mm (5.9in) maximum.

Dimensions: Length (including main armament) 29ft 6in (9.0m); length (hull) 21ft 2in (6.45m); width 10ft 9in (3.27m); height 7ft 10in (2.4m).

Weight: Combat 91,410Ib (41,500kg).

Engine: 12-cylinder, four-stroke, water-cooled, diesel engine developing 630hp at 2,000rpm.

Performance: Road speed 31mph (50km/h); road range with two additional 200l fuel tanks 340 miles (545km); vertical obstacle 2ft 8in (0.8m); trench 8ft 10in (2.7m); gradient 60 percent.

(Data apply to T-55 AM2B.)

The Russian T-54 main battle tank appeared in 1947 and quickly became the Warsaw Pact's first standard MBT. The T-54 was armed with the D-10T 100mm gun and the turret was virtually hemispherical in shape, which gave good ballistic protection, but made it somewhat cramped inside by Western standards. The T-55 appeared in 1960 and incorporated many improvements, including a more powerful engine. It used the same 100mm main gun and the first production model also retained the bow-mounted machine gun although this was deleted from the T-55A onwards. There are many modified versions of the T-54/55 series, the last to be developed for the Russian Army being the T-55 AM2B, which has a new turret, appliqué armor on both turret and hull, a new and more powerful engine, much improved electronics and vision devices, and the same tracks as the T-72.   *Continued over*

Most Iraqi Army T-55s are thought to be entirely of the earlier, unmodified type and their 100mm gun would be completely ineffective against US Army M1A1/M1A2 and British Challengers. It could, however, penetrate the relatively thin armor of infantry fighting vehicles, such as the M1 Bradley and British Warrior, and of course would make mincemeat of soft-skinned vehicles. At least a proportion of the Iraqi T-55s have been given locally developed upgrades, including, in some cases, appliqué armor and in others the installation of a 125mm gun, as used by the T-72.

▲ **Above** *Iraqi T-54s and T-55s were totally defeated by US armor in the 1991 war, and their best chance of any success at all will be as well dug-in, isolated strong points firing at APCs and soft-skinned trucks.*

Type 59 Main Battle Tank

Country of origin: China.

Crew: 4.

Armament: One Type 59 (D-10T copy) 100mm rifled gun; one Type 59T 7.62mm co-axial machine gun; one Type 59T AA 7.652mm machine gun.

Armor: 1.5in-8in (39mm-203mm).

Dimensions: Length (including armament) 29ft 6in (9.00m); length (hull) 19ft 10in (6.04m); width 10ft 8in (3.27m); height 8ft 6in (2.59m).

Weight: Combat 79,300lb (36,000kg).

Ground pressure: 11.38lb/sq in (0.80kg/sq cm).

▲ **Above**   *This cheering Iraqi crew had just driven their T-59 tank into Kuwait in 1990, but their success was short-lived. Like the Soviet T-55 on which it was based, the Type 59 is no match at all for US tank guns.*   *Continued over*

Engine: Model 12150L V-12 liquid-cooled diesel developing 520hp at 2,000rpm.

Performance: Road speed 31mph (50km/h); range 273 miles (440km); vertical obstacle 2ft 7in (0.79m); trench 8ft 10in (2.7m), gradient 60 percent.

When the People's Liberation Army (PLA) defeated Chiang Kai-Shek's Kuomintang in 1949 it quickly established its own MBT production facilities and a small number of T-54s were procured from the then friendly Soviet Union. This model was copied exactly and put into production at a new factory at Baotou, near Peking. Designated the Type 59 by the West, the first production versions reached the PLA in about 1957 and production rose steadily to a rate of some 500-700 per year by the 1970s, peaking at about 1,000 per year in the early 1980s.

The original Type 59 was identical to the Soviet T-54, but the tank was progressively developed during its long production run in China. The producers offer no fewer than eight separate packages to enable current users of the Type 59 or T-54/-55 to upgrade their fleets. These enhancements include everything from appliqué armor, through new optical and electronic devices to either a new-model 100mm gun or a new Chinese-developed 105mm gun, but so far as is known no such kits have been supplied to Iraq.

T-62 Main Battle Tank

Country of origin: Russia.

Crew: 4.

Armament: One U-5TS 115mm gun; one PKT 7.62mm PKT machine gun coaxial with main armament; one DShK 12.7mrn anti-aircraft machine gun.

Armour: 20mm-242mm (0.79in-9.52in).

Dimensions: Length (overall) 30ft 7in (9.33m); length (hull) 21ft 9in (6.63m); width 11ft (3.35m); height (without anti-aircraft machine gun) 7ft 10in (2.4m).

Weight: Combat 88,200lb (40,000kg).

Ground pressure: 11.81b/sq in (0.83kg/sq cm).

▲ **Above** *The Iraqis are known to have upgraded at least some of their T-62 tanks in local army workshops, but how successfully remains to be seen. Despite such programs these tanks will still be no match for US M1 MBT*

Engine: Model V-55-5 12-cylincler water-cooled diesel engine developing 580hp at 2,000rpm.

Performance: Road speed 31mph (50km/h); range (without additional fuel tanks) 280 miles (450km); vertical obstacle 2ft 8in (0.8m); trench 9ft 2in (2.8m); gradient 60 percent.

The T-62 was developed in the late 1950s as the successor to the T-54/T-55 series, and was first seen in public in May 1965. In appearance it is very similar to the earlier T-54, but has a longer and wider hull, a new turret and main armament, and can easily be distinguished from the T-54 since the latter has a distinct gap between its first and second road wheels, whereas the T-62's road wheels are more evenly spaced. Also, the T-62's gun is provided with a bore evacuator. The hull of the T-62 is of all-welded construction with the glacis plate being 4in (10cm) thick. The turret is of cast amor, and this varies in thickness from 6.7in (17cm) at the front to 2.4in (6cm) at the rear. The driver is seated at the front of the hull on the left side, with the other three crew members in the turret, the commander and gunner on the left and the loader on the right. The engine and transmission are at the rear of the hull. The suspension is of the well-tried torsion bar type, and consists of five road wheels with the idler at the front, and the drive sprocket at the rear.

The 115mm U-5TS gun is of the smoothbore type, and has an elevation of +17 degrees. The 115mm round is manually loaded, but once fired the gun automatically returns to a set angle at which the empty cartridge case is ejected from the breech, after which it moves on to a chute and is then thrown out through a small hatch in the turret rear.

There are three variants of the T-62; the T-62M is an improved MBT, the T-62K is a command tank, and the M1977 is an armored recovery vehicle. Some 8,000 T-62s remain in service around the world and many are being upgraded by the addition of new armor, tracks, sideskirts, and guns.

The T-62 is probably the most numerous type in the Iraqi tank fleet, although experience during the 1991 Gulf War showed that its 115mm gun is no match for the M1A1/M1A2 Abrams or Challenger 2, even at ranges under 1,000yd (914m).

▲ **Above** *Designed for combat on the open plains of central Europe, T-62s have been used by many armies around the world, but in many combats in various conflicts they have never outfought US tanks.*

T-72 Main Battle Tank

Country of origin: Russia.

Crew: 3.

Armament: One 2A46 125mm gun; one PKT 7.62mm co-axial machine gun; one NSVT 12.7mrn anti-aircraft machine gun.

Armor: composite.

Dimensions: Length (including main armament) 30ft 4in (9.24m); length (hull) 22ft 10in (6.95m); width 15ft 7in (4.75m); height 7ft 10in (2.37m).

Weight: Combat 90,310lb (41,000kg).

Ground pressure: 11.80lb/sq in (0.83kg/sq cm).

Engine: V-12 diesel engine developing 780hp at 2,000rpm.

▲ **Above** *The T-72 is the most modern tank in the Iraqi Army and all examples have been handed over to the Revolutionary Guards. Whether they will fight them any better than in 1991 is very doubtful.*

Performance: Road speed 50mph (80km/h); road range 300 miles (483km); vertical obstacle 2ft 8in (0.85m); trench 8ft 10in (2.7m); gradient 60 percent.

The T-72 entered production in 1971 and was in wide-scale service with the Soviet Army by 1973, although it was not reported publicly by Western experts until 1977. The driver is seated centrally under a well-sloped glacis plate, while the other two crew members are in the turret, commander on the right, gunner on the left. There is an automatic loader with a horizontal feed system. The 125mm smoothbore main gun is fitted with a light alloy thermal sleeve and a fume extractor, and fires three types of ammunition. The theoretical rate of fire is 8 rounds per minute, although whether this could be achieved, let alone sustained, on the battlefield is a different matter.

Iraq is known to have imported some 500 T-72s from the (then) USSR in the mid- and late-1980s. At a defense exposition in 1989 the Iraqis announced that they were assembling the Assad Babyle (Lion of Babylon) MBT, which was essentially the T-72M1, but armed with a locally produced 125mm main gun. Some of these were also fitted with a decoy system, designed to mislead optically tracked, wire-guided anti-tank weapons, such as the US Army's TOW. During the build-up to the Gulf War, President Saddam realized that defeat was inevitable and reallocated these T-72M1s to his Republican Guard and withdrew them well into Iraq to insure their survival. Some of the unmodified versions did take part in the battles with the Coalition forces, but were not particularly successful; despite this, it remains the Iraqi's most effective MBT.

▲ **Above** *When it appeared in the 1970s the Soviet T-72 was an unusual and exciting design. It is now very dated and its one chance of success might be if used in vast numbers, which the Iraqis do not have.*

M1A1/M1A2 Abrams Main Battle Tank

Country of origin: United States.

Crew: 4.

Armament: One M256 Rheinmetall 120mm smoothbore gun (105mm gun in M1); one M240 7.62mm co-axial machine gun; one M2 12.7mm; one M240 7.62mm anti-aircraft machine gun.

Armor: Classified.

Dimensions: Length (gun forward) 32.3ft (9.8m); length (hull) 25.9ft (7.9m); width 11.9ft (3.7m); height 9.5ft (2.9m).

Weight: Combat 125,890lb (57,154kg).

Ground pressure: 13.65lb/sq in (0.96kg/sq cm).

Engine: Textron Lycoming AGT-1500 gas-turbine; 1,500bhp at 30,000rpm.

Performance: Road speed 41mph (67km/h), range 300 miles (480km); vertical obstacle 3.5ft (1.1m); trench 9.0ft (2.74); gradient 60 percent.

(Data for M1A2.)

The M1 forms the central pillar of the military might of the US Army and is also a vital element of the power of the Marine Corps. Its powerful gun and exceptional mobility enable it to provide the mobile firepower for armored units and it can outfight any MBT in any other army in the world, by day or by night, and in any weather. It also provides armored protection for its crew in any combat environment they are likely to encounter on the modern battlefield.

▲ **Above** *US Army M1 MBTs can out-shoot, out-maneuver and out-pace any tank the Iraqis possess, and in the event that the enemy fires at these tanks the incoming rounds will simply bounce off the special armor.* *Continued over*

The M1 exists in four versions: M1, M1 (Improved), M1A1 and M1A2. The initial production version was the M1, armed with a 105mm gun, of which 2,674 were built, with the last 300 having better armored protection and being designated M1 (Improved). A major advance was made with M1A1, produced from 1985 through 1993, with the M1's 105mm main gun being replaced by the Rheinmetall 120mm smoothbore gun and numerous other enhancements, including an improved suspension, new turret, increased armor protection, and a nuclear-biological-chemical protection system. A total of 403 M1A1s were also built for the US Marine Corps, and are virtually identical to the Army's M1A1, except that they have a Deep Water Fording Kit for use in amphibious landings. The latest M1A2 series includes all of the M1A1 features, plus an independent commander's station incorporating a thermal viewer, new navigation equipment, a digital data-bus and a radio interface unit which links all M1A2s on the battlefield to give them a common battlefield picture. A total of 77 new M1A2s have been built, but approximately 1,000 of the original M1s are being rebuilt to this latest standard.

The main armament in the M1 is the 105mm gun, which was developed in the United Kingdom and produced under license in the United States. But the main weapon of the M1A1 and M1A2 is the M256 120mm smoothbore cannon, which was designed by the Rheinmetall Corporation of Germany and is also being built in the United States. In both cases, the main gun can be aimed and fired while the tank is on the move, with either the commander or the gunner selecting a target, following which the gunner uses the laser rangefinder to take the range and then depresses the firing switch. The computer makes all the necessary calculations and adjustments required to ensure a first-round hit. Secondary armament comprises a coaxial 7.62mm machine gun and two

▲ **Above** *The main gun on this M1A2 is the German-designed but US-built M256 smoothbore 120mm cannon which can destroy any Iraqi tank before it gets anywhere near the range of its own gun*

machine guns mounted on the turret roof, a 12.7mm machine gun at the commander's station and a 7.62mm machine gun at the loader's station. Depending on the version, the tank carries either 55 rounds of 105mm or 40 rounds of 120mm, plus 1,000 rounds of 12.7mm and 11,400 rounds of 7.62mm machine gun ammunition. Nuclear, biological and chemical (NBC) warfare protection is provided by an overpressure clean-air conditioning air system, a radiological warning system, and a chemical agent detector. The crew are individually equipped with protective suits and masks.

The M1 is powered by the Textron Lycoming AGT-1500 gas-turbine, with a fully automatic transmission, equipped with four forward and two reverse gears. The two prime measures of battlefield agility are the power-to-weight ratio, which in the case of the M1 is very high, 27hp/tonne, and acceleration, where the M1 is capable of reaching 20mph (32km/h) from a standing start in six seconds. Prolonged service use has also demonstrated that the AGT-1500 is very reliable, mechanically simple and particularly easy to service. On the other hand, it is definitely noisy (acoustic signature), emits a very hot exhaust (strong infra-red signature), and is thirsty on fuel, although the logistic support during Desert Storm was so effective that this was not a problem.

The first battle test for the M1 came in Operations Desert Shield/Desert Storm when it faced some 500 modern T-72s, about 1,600 older T-62s and about 700 1950s vintage T-54s. US forces fielded 1,848 MBTs during the campaign, of which the majority were M1A1, but some were the M1A1(HA) (= heavy armor) version. Prior to the land advance Allied air power destroyed some 50 percent of the Iraqi tanks, but as soon as the Abrams were unleashed they quickly dealt with the remainder in their sector, destroying large numbers of enemy while incurring only 18 battle losses, of which nine were permanent and nine were repaired. Not one crewman was lost. The US Army's fleet comprises: M1 – 2,674, all to be converted to M1A2; M1 Improved – 894; M1A1 – 4,796; M1A2 – 77 new-build completed, with M1s being upgraded. The Marine Corps has 403 M1A1s.

RECONNAISSANCE AND SURVEILLANCE

Once hostilities have started in any war it is essential for commanders at all levels to have a constant flow of information about the enemy, in order to assess his current deployment and future intentions, and, in the shorter term, to find targets for air strikes and artillery engagement. This will certainly be the case for the United States forces, who will have non-stop inputs from a wide variety of sources and sensors, including satellites, reconnaissance aircraft, UAVs, electronic warfare units, radar, helicopters, espionage, and so on, and will also put a major effort into preventing the Iraqis from gaining information.

The Iraqi Army's ground reconnaissance assets are paltry, to say the least, and they have been unable to make good any of the very grave deficiencies exposed in the 1991 war. There are a few locally built UAVs and a few Cymbeline mortar-

▲ **Above** *Global Hawk has an intercontinental range and a 36-hour endurance; it is able to observe Iraqi targets in almost complete safety.*

locating radars may survive from the 1980s.

The only real assets are some 400 scout cars, of four different types. The Brazilian defense industry was surprisingly successful in export markets in the 1970s and '80s, and one of their best customers was Iraq.

Among the items bought were 300 Jararaca EE3 armored scout cars. These are 4 x 4 vehicles, with a pointed bow, well-sloped glacis plate, a central compartment for the crew and a rear-mounted Mercedes-Benz diesel engine. Various armaments can be fitted, including a 12.7mm machine gun, Milan anti-tank guided missile and a 20mm cannon.

The second Brazilian armored car is the Cascavel EE9, of which Iraq purchased no fewer than 750 in the late 1970s. This is a six-wheeled vehicle with a Mercedes-Benz engine driving the rear four wheels. Main armament is a turret-mounted Cockerill 90mm gun.

Iraq also operates the French AML-90 (= *AutoMitrailleuse Légère*), 70 of which were delivered in the 1960s. This is a light, fast, long-ranged and cheap 4 x 4 vehicle, and its 90mm cannon gives it a respectable offensive capability.

Fourth in these types of vehicle is the BRDM-2, which was the standard reconnaissance vehicle of the Soviet Army from the mid-1960s onwards and was also widely exported. It is a 4 x 4 vehicle with a four-man crew and is usually armed with either a single 14.5mm KPVT heavy machine gun in a turret or four AT-2 Sagger anti-tank missiles under a protective cover. These are likely to prove less than adequate.

On the other side, the United States forces have a plethora of reconnaissance and surveillance systems, almost none of which is vulnerable to Iraqi counter-attacks. These range from satellites to remotely monitored ground sensors, but the RQ-1 Predator UAV illustrates the degree of sophistication currently available to American ground commanders.

▲ **Above** *Unlike the US forces with their vast numbers of different types of surveillance systems, the Iraqi Army is restricted to visual means, from such as this Soviet-supplied wheeled scout car; no contest!*

" ...the United States forces have a plethora of reconnaissance and surveillance systems, almost none of which is vulnerable to Iraqi counter-attacks. "

RQ-1 Predator UAV

Manufacturer: General Atomics Aeronautical Systems Inc.

Type: Long-range surveillance reconnaissance and target acquisition UAV.

Weight: Empty 950lb (43kg); maximum take-off 2,250lb (1,021kg).

Dimensions: Length 27.0ft (8.2m); height 6.9ft (2.1m); wingspan 48.7ft (14.8m).

Engine: Rotax 912 four-cylinder engine; 81hp.

Performance: Cruise speed 70-120kt (84-140mph/135-225km/h); range 400nm (454 miles/731km/h); 16 hours on station; ceiling 25,000ft (7,620m).

Launch and recovery: Runway, wheeled.

Armament: See notes.

Payload: 450lb (204kg).

(Data for RQ-1A.)

▼ **Below** *UAVs are playing an increasingly important role in US surveillance operations and have been of special importance over Afghanistan. They are also capable of carrying deadly weapons, such as Hellfire missiles.*

The RQ-1 Predator is a USAF-operated system which is normally employed in moderate risk areas. Each system comprises four airborne platforms with their related sensors, a ground control station (GCS), a satellite communication suite and 55 people, all of which must be collocated on the same airfield, where the aircraft, which is quite large, requires a hard surface runway measuring 5,000 x 125ft (1,524 x 38m). The aircraft carries three cameras transmitting full motion video, one in the nose, which is normally used by the flight controller, a daylight

Continued over

TV camera and a low light/night infrared camera, together with a synthetic aperture radar for looking through smoke, clouds or haze. The cameras produce full motion video and the synthetic aperture radar produces still-frame radar images. The UAV and its sensors are controlled by the GCS; manned by four people, this is mounted in a shelter and is the largest single component in the system; it is air-transportable in a C-130.

The satellite suite consists of a 20ft (6.1m) satellite dish and associated support equipment, which provides communications between the ground station and the aircraft when it is beyond line-of-sight and also links into networks disseminating secondary intelligence. The RQ-1 can operate at 25,000ft (7,620m), but typically flies at around 15,000ft (4,570m), with a normal mission involving a 400nm transit, followed by 14 hours on station.

In April 2001, the U.S. Air Force tested a Predator armed with three Hellfire anti-armor missiles. All tests were carried out with the Predator flying at a height of 2,000ft (610m), a speed of 70kt (80mph/130km/h) and at a range of about 3 miles (5km). The first two trial shots used missiles with inert warheads, the target being illuminated first by a ground-based laser and then by the Predator's own laser designator. On both being successful, a third engagement using the Predator's laser-designator and a missile with a live warhead resulted in a direct hit. The next step in this particular program is to increase the Hellfire launch altitude from 2,000ft to 15,000ft, where there is much less chance of the UAV being shot down. There are current proposals to adapt the Predator to carry either 12 Hellfire missiles or short-range, heat-seeking AIM-9 Sidewinder missiles against such targets as helicopters and low-flying aircraft.

A separate development of the original Predator is the I-Gnat, which is used by the CIA, and one of which was shot down over Afghanistan. It is believed that it was one of these aircraft that was involved in the incident in Yemen in November 2002, in which a car carrying wanted men (suspected al-Qaeda terrorists) was destroyed by a UAV-launched missile and the occupants killed.

▼ **Below** *The Predator is operated by the USAF and the CIA. It was one of these craft, armed with Hellfire missiles, that attacked and killed an al-Qaeda leader and five comrades in Yemen on 5 November, 2002.*

ARMORED INFANTRY WARFARE

Most of Iraq, particularly in the center and south, is what generals refer to as "good tank country," with vast areas of open space, few centers of population and a lack of major topographical features which would interfere with the fighting. As a result, the United States advance will generally be led by the tanks with the armored infantry in support, but ready to take the lead if the tactical situation should require it.

The United States operates a homogenous fleet of M2 Bradley vehicles, with a number of M113 APCs in secondary roles. Against this the Iraqi Army has a fleet of BMP-1/-2 fighting vehicles and a motley array of tracked and wheeled APCs. The BMPs are described separately, but the

APCs, of which there are some 2,400, are of at least ten types from five different countries, which would pose logistical problems at the best of times, but must be a nightmare under the UN sanctions regime. They are also a mix of wheeled and tracked types.

The oldest APCs in service are some BTR-152, six-wheeled, open-top vehicles, dating back to the 1950s and probably retained simply for lack of anything better. Of more recent Russian origin is the 8 x 8 BTR-60, an open-topped vehicle with a boat-shaped hull, but without overhead protection for the squad, who must jump over the sides to debus, making the situation in combat particularly hazardous.

Iraq's Czech-built OT-64 (also known as the SKOT-2A) is similar in concept to the BTR-60, in that it is an eight-wheeled, open-top APC, but is a quite different design, being based on the successful Tatra T-813 eight-ton truck. It is also one of the largest APCs in service in any army, carrying a crew of two and 15 infantrymen.

▲ **Above**   *The Iraqi Army operates a wide variety of APCs including some of these MT-LBs; they are intended to protect infantry from artillery shell splinters but are of no use under US air attack, which will be constant.*

> **"Iraq's oldest APCs are some BTR-152, six-wheeled, open-top vehicles, dating back to the 1950s and probably retained simply for lack of anything better."**

Finally, there is the Brazilian Urutu, a six-wheeled vehicle, weighing 14 tons and carrying a crew of two and a squad of 11 men. Iraq received a total of 500 in the 1980s.

The Iraqis operate an equally bewildering variety of tracked APCs, starting with the elderly Russian BTR-50 and its Czech-built derivative, the OT-62, which are tracked vehicles with a troop compartment, accommodating a squad of 12 infantrymen; this is open-topped in the Soviet vehicle and with a light armored cover in the Czech version.

The MT-LB is a tracked APC produced in the USSR in the 1960s and '70s in parallel with the BMP-1. It is a cheap and simple vehicle, very low in overall height and with a particularly low ground-pressure. It carries a crew of two plus 11 troops or 2 tons of cargo.

Iraq's Chinese-built YW-701 is a tracked armored command and communication vehicle, which was a 1960s development of the YW-531 APC. It has a raised rear compartment, housing radios and staff officers, and is employed at the headquarters of armored and mechanized units and formations of the Iraqi Army. A small number of M113 APCs were captured from the Iranians in the 1980s war. These are noted for their simplicity and reliability, but even so the absence of spares must make continued operation very difficult.

> **"The Iraqis operate an equally bewildering variety of tracked APCs..."**

▲ **Above**   *Another type of APC available in small numbers to the Iraqi Army is the Czech-built OT-64 eight-wheeled vehicle. Highly regarded when it entered service in the 1960s, it is now obsolete.*

BRADLEY M2/M3 IFV/CFV

Manufacturer: United Defense, USA.

Type: M2 – Infantry Fighting Vehicle (IFV); M3 – Cavalry Fighting Vehicle (CFV).

Crew: M2 – 3 crew, 7 infantry; M2A2 – 3 crew, 6 infantry; M3 – 3 crew, 2 scouts.

Armament: One 25mm cannon (chain-gun); one 7.62 mm coaxial machine gun; one twin-tube TOW missile launcher.

Armor: Welded aluminum/spaced laminate armor.

Dimensions: Length 21.3ft (6.5m); width 11.8ft (3.6m); height 9.8ft (3.0m).

Weight: 50,000lb (22,680kg).

Engine: Cummins VTA-903T, water-cooled, 4-stroke diesel; 506bhp,

Performance: Road speed 41mph (66km/h); road range 300 miles (483km); water speed 4.5mph (7.2km/h).

The US infantry will all move in M2 Bradley IFVs, while the ground reconnaissance parties will be mounted in its close kin, the M3 CFV. The role of the M2 IFV is to move infantry about the battlefield, to provide covering fire to dismounted troops, and to suppress enemy tanks, other fighting vehicles and soft-skinned transport. To achieve this the M2 carries three crew, plus six fully equipped infantrymen. The M3 performs scouting missions, for which it carries three crew plus two scouts.

▲ **Above**   *In contrast to the Iraqi IFVs and APCs, the US M2 Bradley IFV is at the cutting edge of modern technology: fast, agile, well-armed, with good armored protection – and it carries a well-armed seven-man squad.*   *Continued over*

The M2/M3 vehicles are constructed of welded aluminum armor, reinforced in critical areas by spaced laminated armor plates. They are divided into three main areas: driving compartment, turret and infantry compartment. The vehicle is powered by a Cummins VTA-903T turbo-diesel with a Lockheed Martin HMPT-500 hydromechanical transmission and the reliability of this system has far exceeded initial expectations, with only three vehicles (out of 2,200 deployed) being disabled during Operation Desert Storm. The M2/M3 has excellent cross-country capability and is fully able to keep pace with the M1 Abrams MBT in all types of terrain. The driver is equipped with four periscopes, three facing forward and one to the left. The central periscope can be replaced by an image intensifier for night driving.

Main armament is a Boeing (McDonnell Douglas) M242 25mm Bushmaster "chain gun" which has a single barrel with an integrated dual feed mechanism and remote feed selection. An M240C 7.62mm machine gun is mounted coaxially to the right of the Bushmaster. A twin-tube Raytheon BGM-71 TOW anti-tank missile launcher is mounted on the left side of the turret. A twin-wire command link is dispensed from the missile in flight, enabling the gunner to control the missile up to impact on the target. Maximum range is 4,155yd (3.8km). Unlike the chain gun, the TOW can be launched and controlled only while the vehicle is stationary.

The M3 CFV is identical to the M2 IFV except that instead of carrying six infantry in the rear compartment it carries a pair of scouts, for whom there are no external firing ports. It also carries additional radios and ammunition, including TOW Dragon or Javelin missiles. The M2A2/M3A2 upgrade program is currently in progress and involves fitting additional appliqué steel armor, with provision for explosive reactive armor (ERA), if tactically necessary, to provide increased protection against HEAT (shaped charge) weapons.

▲ **Above** *A US soldier dismounted from his M3 Bradley CFV to launch a Stinger air defense missile, just one of the many weapons systems available to the troops manning this flexible and capable vehicle.*

BMP-1/-2 Armored Infantry Fighting Vehicle

Country of origin: Russia.

Crew: BMP-1 – 3 + 8; BMP-2 – 3 + 7.

Armament: BMP-1 – 1 x 73mm smoothbore gun, 40 rounds; AT~3 (NATO = Sagger) ATGW launcher; 7.62PKT (co-axial), 1,000 rounds; BMP-2 – one 30mm cannon, one machine gun; four AT-5 Spandrel ATGW.

Armor: Mainly 14mm.

Dimensions: Length 22ft 6in (6.86m); width 10ft 1in (3.09m); height 6ft 10in (2.08m).

Weight: laden in combat, 14.4 tons (14,600kg).

Engine: Model 5D-20 V-6 six-in-line water-cooled diesel, 257hp.

Performance: Road speed 50mph (80km/h); water 5mph (8km/h); range 310 miles (500km).

(Data for BMP-2 unless noted.)

Iraqi armored infantry will move in the BMP-1 and -2 IFVs which, while fine vehicles in their day, are now somewhat dated and are, in any case, poorly maintained. Iraq has a fleet of just under 1,000 tracked AIFVs, a mixture of BMP-1s and -2s, all supplied by the Soviet Union before 1991.

The BMP-1 has a vehicle crew of three: commander (who is also commander of the dismounted infantry section), driver, and gunner. Both crew and passengers have nuclear/biological/chemical warfare protection in the pressurized hull, and air filters are fitted as standard. When it was first seen in 1967 Western defense experts were very envious, since although smaller than the West's own APCs it had greater firepower and the eight troops had periscopes enabling them to fire on the move.

▲ **Above** *The BMP-1 (seen here) and BMP-2 (with 30mm cannon and im-proved missiles) were both Russian designs and were highly-respected, not least in the West, when they first appeared – which was a long time ago.*

The 73mm low-pressure gun has a smooth bore and fires fin-stabilized HEAT rounds, the automatic loader giving a firing rate of eight rounds per minute. The missile launcher above the gun carries one round ready to fire, and three more rounds are carried inside the vehicle, In addition, one of the infantrymen inside the vehicle normally carries an SA-7 Grail SAM.

The BMP-1 is also fully amphibious, being propelled in the water by its tracks. A full range of night-vision equipment is fitted, although only the old-fashioned active infra-red types have been seen so far, which is, of course, easily detected on a modern battlefield.   *Continued over*

During the 1973 Yom Kippur war the Egyptians used their BMPs exactly as taught in the Soviet tactical textbooks with disastrous results. The idea of a MICV charging onto enemy positions with all armament blazing away – including the infantrymen's rifles firing through ports – made a nice theory, but proved totally unworkable in practice. As a result the whole concept of the use of BMP was revised.

Nevertheless, the Iraqis are very unlikely to use their BMPs in aggressive tactics, except, perhaps, for very local counter-attacks. Instead, they are more likely to be used in transporting soldiers to new positions, mostly rearwards.

▼ **Below** *If handled with determination and skill, this BMP-2 might be adequate, but it is doubtful that the Iraqi Army has good junior leaders, even in the much-vaunted Republican Guard.*

BATTLEFIELD AVIATION

Iraqi Helicopters

All Iraqi military helicopters are operated by the Army and the total current fleet is estimated to comprise some 380 aircraft, of which about 150 are armed and the remainder are used for transporting troops or cargo. However, all helicopters are very complicated machines and even the very rugged Soviet-built types require a great deal of maintenance and spare parts to keep them flying, while the pilots need constant training to insure their competence. Thus, while there may be about 380 airframes, the actual availability, even in a crisis, is likely to be very much fewer. A November 2002 TV news program, for example, showed a reporter on a flight in an Iraqi military Mi-8 Hip, which was in such a poor state that no Western army or air force would have allowed it to fly, let alone take passengers.

The most potent attack helicopters operated by the Iraqi Army are the survivors of at least 40 Mil Mi-24 Hinds supplied by the Soviet Union in the 1980s. These are the only special-to-role attack helicopters and the remainder are armed aircraft which were supplied already equipped to launch missiles. These include the German MBB Bo-105 and the French SA-316 Alouette and SA-342 Gazelle, all of which can launch anti-tank guided missiles such as AS-11 and HOT. A rather unusual type is the French SA-321H Super Frelon, of which 16 were acquired fitted to launch Exocet anti-ship missiles for use in the so-called "tanker war" in the 1980s. Some of these still remain and pose a threat to shipping in northern Gulf waters, although there is no record of them having been so employed during the 1991 Gulf War. The Iraqis

also acquired 45 Bell 214STs in 1987-88; these were ostensibly for civil use but were impressed into the military as soon as they were delivered and are reported to be armed with machine guns and possibly also with missiles.

Iraq's transport helicopter fleet is potentially somewhat larger. Over 100 Russian-built Mil Mi-8/-17 Hips were supplied in the 1970s and '80s and it would seem reasonably certain that a significant number survive. Iraq also received some of the giant Mil Mi-6 Hook-A from the USSR and a very small number might survive, kept going because of their lifting capacity, although their large size makes maintenance particularly difficult. The remainder are a somewhat mixed bag comprising: Agusta AS-61 and AB-212, German MBB BK-117 and some Hughes 300/500.

Mi-24 Hind

Manufacturer: Mil, Russia.

Type: Attack helicopter.

Weight: Empty 18,740lb (8,500kg); normal take-off with maximum internal load 24,470lb (11,100kg); maximum take-off 27,557lb (12,500kg).

Dimensions: Length, fuselage 57.4ft (17.5m), length overall, rotors turning 70/9ftft (21.6m); wingspan 21.3ft | (6.5m); height 13.9ft (4.2m); rotor diameter 56.8ft (17.3m).

Powerplant: Two Klimov (Isotov) TV3-117 turbines, each 2,200shp (1,640kW).

Performance: Maximum level speed, clean, at optimum altitude 168kt (192mph/310km/h); cruising speed at optimum altitude 140kt (162mh/260km/h); range, normal 405nm (466 miles/759km); combat radius, normal fuel 86nm (99 miles/160km), with auxiliary fuel tanks 135nm (155 miles/250km); service ceiling 14,763ft (4,500m); vertical climb rate 50ft/sec (15m/sec).

Payload: Internal load 8 combat troops or 4 litters; external (with weapons) 3,307lb (1,500kg); external (no weapons) 5,511lb (2,500kg).

Armament: One 4-barrel 12.7mm Gatling-type machine gun (turret-mounted); 57mm rockets; AT-2C (Swatter) ATGMs.

Crew: Two (pilot/commander, gunner/observer/copilot).

(Data for Mil Mi-24D.)

This is, without a doubt, the only Iraqi battlefield helicopter that might cause the US forward troops some concern, although the actual numbers will be small and the attrition rate is likely to be high. The original Mil Mi-24 (NATO = Hind-A, -B, -C) helicopters were developed by the Soviet Air Force as flying armored personnel carriers and were created essentially by adding a new two-man cockpit to the engines, dynamic components and eight-man troop-carrying cabin of the very successful Mil Mi-8 (NATO = Hip), with the addition of stub wings which carried rocket and guided missile launchers. The prototype flew in 1970 and it was produced in some numbers in three closely related versions. The growing importance of the anti-tank role, however, led to a major redesign, resulting in the Mil-24D (Hind-D), which rapidly became one of the most influential battlefield aircraft of the 1980s and 1990s. It was deployed throughout the Warsaw Pact and also became the most notorious aircraft of the Afghanistan War. It has many of the characteristics of its contemporary, the American AH-64 Apache, but with the added capability of being able to transport eight troops, if required.

The Hind-D has tandem bubble canopies for the pilot and gunner, with a 12.7mm YaKB machine gun in a chin-mounted turret and six hardpoints, three under each wing. A considerable variety of stores can be carried, but a typical load would be eight AT-6 ATGMs, and two 57mm rocket pods. Extra ammunition can be carried in the cargo compartment. There is considerable emphasis on survivability: all aircraft have an over-pressurization system for NBC operations, and both the armored cockpits and rotor head are constructed of titanium and are intended to withstand 20mm cannon hits.

The stub wings provide some 25percent of the total lift in forward flight, although there is a problem in that in a low-speed, steeply banked turn, the inner wing can lose its lift, but not the outer wing, which leads to excessive roll. This has to be countered by increasing airspeed, and this, coupled with the Hind's size and weight, reduce its maneuverability, which results in them normally being operated in pairs, for mutual protection.

Continued over

▲ **Above** *Much-feared in the Russian war in Afghanistan, the Mi-24 Hind is one of the most potent attack helicopters in the world. A small number are in service with the Iraqis, but they will not last long before being shot down.*

United States Helicopters

The US Army will take a large fleet of helicopters to the Gulf. This will include AH-64 Apache attack helicopters, OH-58 Kiowa Warrior scouts, UH-60 Blackhawk utility, and CH-47 Chinook transports. The actual numbers will depend on the command decision as to the size of force required. These are well-tested designs, all of which took part in the 1991 Gulf War and have been progressively modified since to incorporate the lessons of that campaign.

▼ **Below**   *The gunner mans a 7.62mm minigun at the cabin door of an MH-60 operated by the US Army's Special Operations Command 160th Special Operations Aviation Regiment.*

◄ **Left**   *US helicopters, like this USMC AH-1W, are well maintained, something denied to Iraqi machines, which will not last long in battle.*

AH-64 Apache and Longbow

Manufacturer: Boeing (McDonnell Douglas), USA.

Type: Attack helicopter.

Weight: Empty 11,015lb (4,996kg); primary mission gross weight 14,694lb (6,665kg); maximum take-off 17,650lb (8,006kg).

Dimensions: Length 48.1ft (14.7m); height 16.8ft (5.1m); rotor diameter 48.0ft (14.6m).

Powerplant: Two General Electric T700-GE-701 turboshafts, each 1,696shp (1,265kW).

Performance: Maximum airspeed 228mph (365km/h); cruising182mph (293km/h); hover ceiling (IGE) 13,400ft (4,084m), (OGE) 10,200ft (3,109m); maximum range (internal fuel) 428nm (689km); g limits +3.5 to -0.5.

Armament: (see notes).

Crew: Two (pilot and copilot/gunner).

(Data for US Army AH-64D.)

▲ **Above** *AH-64D Apache Longbows will operate deep into Iraq, taking advantage of their agility and heavy weapons fit to deal with any opposition, as they open the way for the advance by ground troops.*

The US Army has more than 800 Apaches in service, of which a large number will be sent to the Gulf to take part in the campaign there. The Apache was first used in combat in 1989 in the US military action in Panama, and later played a very successful part in the 1991 Gulf War.

It has also supported low intensity and peacekeeping operations worldwide, including in northern Iraq, Bosnia and Kosovo.

The US Army version of the AH-64 is powered by two General Electric T700-GE-701C gas-turbine engines, rated at 1,890shp each, enabling the aircraft to cruise at a speed of 145mph (233km/h) with a flight endurance in excess of three hours. Combat radius is approximately 93 statute miles (150km), but the addition of a single external 230gal fuel tank enables this to be extended to some 186 miles (300km), although this is dependent upon a number of factors, including weather, temperature, and payload. Ferry range on internal fuel is 430 miles (690km), but this can be considerably extended by the addition of up to four 230gal external tanks. The AH-64 is air transportable in the C-5, C-141 and C-17.

The AH-64D Longbow Apache is equipped with the Northrop Grumman millimeter-wave Longbow radar, which incorporates an integrated radar frequency interferometer for passive location and identification of radar emitting threats. This operates in the millimeter band which insures not only that it is unaffected by poor visibility or ground clutter, but also, because of its very narrow beamwidth, that it is resistant to countermeasures. Primary weapon system is the Lockheed Martin/Boeing AGM-114D Longbow Hellfire air-to-surface missile which has a millimeter-wave seeker to allow the missile to perform in full fire-and-forget mode. Missile range is 5-7.5miles. The Apache can also be armed with air-to-air missiles (Stinger, Sidewinder, Mistral and Sidearm) and 2.75in rockets. The Longbow Apache carries the combination of armaments necessary for the particular mission and in the close support role a typical loadout would be 16 Hellfire missiles on four 4-rail launchers and four air-to-air missiles. A 30mm automatic Boeing M230 Chain Gun is located under the fuselage. It provides a rate of fire of 625 rounds per minute, and the helicopter can carry up to 1,200 rounds of ammunition.

The Longbow Apache can effect an attack in thirty seconds. The radar dome is unmasked for a single radar scan and then remasked. The processors determine the location, speed and direction of travel of a maximum of 256 targets. The Target Acquisition Designation Sight (AN/ASQ-170) and the Pilot Night Vision Sensor (AN/AAQ-11) were developed by Lockheed Martin. The turret-mounted TADS provides direct view optics, television and three fields of view forward looking infra-red (FLIR) to carry out search, detection and recognition, and Litton laser rangefinder/designator. PNVS consists of a FLIR in a rotating turret located on the nose above the TADS. The image from the PNVS is displayed in the monocular eyepiece of the Honeywell integrated Helmet And Display Sighting System, HADDS, worn by the pilot and copilot/gunner.

▲ **Above**   *A tactic that was developed during Desert Storm and will be used again is to establish helicopter operating bases deep inside Iraqi territory; AH-64s will be crucial to the success of such a base.*

IRAQI ARTILLERY

Towed Artillery

The Iraqi leadership and Army have a particular fixation with artillery. This saw its most extreme realization in the development of Dr. Gerald Bull's "Super Gun" which would have enabled very large caliber shells to be fired from very long tubes direct into Iran, Israel and Saudi Arabia. Today, Iraq manufactures a Yugoslav version of the Soviet 122mm D-30 towed howitzer designated the "Saddam" and also produces a certain amount of artillery ammunition.

The Iraqi Army is estimated to have some 1,900 towed artillery pieces and about 150 self-propelled guns. In the towed category the smallest are the Italian 105mm M-56 pack howitzer and three Russian-designed 122mm caliber weapons: the World War Two vintage M-1938 and the post-war D-30 and D-74. Some of the D-30s were supplied direct from the USSR, some from Yugoslavia and some are claimed to have been manufactured in Iraq as the 122mm Saddam howitzer.

The Russian-made 130mm M46 and its Chinese copy, the 130mm Type 59-1, are both used in the role for which they were designed – counter-battery fire. They are

▲ **Above**   One of many Soviet weapons used by Iraqi artillery, the 122mm D-30 is highly rated, having a good performance for its caliber

▲ **Above**   Towed artillery leaves Iraqi crews woefully exposed to US counterbattery fire and to their own CW/BW agents, if used by Saddam.

Caliber	Weapon	Origin	Range (miles)	Rate of fire (sustained)	Crew	Iraqi towed artillery
105mm	M-56	Italy	6.6	3rpm	7	
122mm	M-1938	USSR	7.4	5rpm	8	
	D-30	USSR	9.6	4rpm	7	
	D-74	USSR	15	3rpm	10	
130mm	M-46	USSR	17.2	3rpm	9	
	Type 59-1	China	17.1	5rpm	7	
155mm	G-5	S. Africa	18.7	2rpm	8	
	GHN-45	Austria	18.7*	6rpm	8	
	M-114	USA	9.1	1.5rpm	1	

* 23.7 miles base-bleed; 26.2 miles RAP.

considered to be highly effective and very accurate weapons, and a battery is normally co-located with radio direction-finding equipment to give them very rapid response.

Largest of the towed weapons are a small number of 155mm G-5 from South Africa, and the Austrian GHN-45, which has the exceptional range of 26+miles (42km) with a rocket-assisted projectile (RAP). There are also a few US-built M-114s, captured during the war against Iran.

Iraqi Self-propelled Artillery

Self-propelled (SP) artillery pieces are of much greater value on the modern battlefield, but Iraq has comparatively few, possibly about 150, although some ad hoc weapons may have been extemporized by mounting artillery tubes on surplus tracked chassis. The known assets include three types supplied to Iraq in the 1970s and '80s. These are the Soviet 122mm 2S1 (M-1974) and the 152mm (M-1973) 2S3, both efficient weapons of good performance. There are also the survivors of 85 155mm AUF-1s bought from France in the early 1980s. Finally, there may be a few of the remaining US-built 155mm M109A1/A2, captured from Iran during the 1980-88 war.

Caliber	Weapon	Origin	Range (miles)	Rate of fire (sustained)	Crew
122mm	2S1	USSR	9.6	3rpm	4
152mm	2S3	USSR	15	2rpm	5
155mm	M109A1/A2	USA	9.2	4rpm	6
	AUF-1(GCT)	France	13.1	4rpm	4

Iraqi self-propelled artillery

US Towed Artilleery

The US Army and Marine Corps also use towed artillery in scenarios where their lack of protection of operators against shell splinters and chemical/biological weapons is considered to be less important than their lightness and air transportability. Heaviest is the 155mm M198, which is towed by a 5-ton truck and has a maximum range with a normal shell of 24,500yd (22,400m). In the war with Iraq this would probably be found only with Marine Corps units.

The other weapon is the 105mm M119A1 105mm howitzer, which can be carried by a helicopter as an underslung load and is usually towed by an HMMWV. It fires a normal shell to 15,315yd (14,000m), but has a rocket-assisted projectile (RAP) which increases range to 20,785yd (19,000m). This would be found in Army airborne units, if they were deployed.

▲ **Above**   *The US Army uses towed artillery in light/airborne divisions.*

▶ **Right**   *M198 155mm howitzer is used by some USMC artillery units*

155mm Self-Propelled Howitzer M109A6 (Paladin)

Manufacturer: Team Paladin (United Defense), USA.

Type: Self-propelled howitzer.

Crew: 4.

Armament: M284 155mm/39 caliber howitzer, 39 projectiles; one 0.5in (12.7mm) M2HB machine gun.

Dimensions: Length overall (howitzer forward) 32.0ft (9.8m); length, hull 22. 6ft (6.9m); width, hull 12.9ft (3.9m).

Weight: Combat 63,600lb (28,800kg).

Engine: General Motors 8V71T, 8-cylinder, 2-cycle, V-8, supercharged diesel, 345bhp at 2,300rpm.

Performance – vehicle: Road speed 38mph (61km/h); road range 186 miles (300km); maximum gradient 60 percent; maximum side slope 40 percent; vertical obstacle 1.8ft (0.5m); trench 6.0ft (1.8m).

▲ **Above** *The US Army's M190A6 Paladin is very mobile, has good range, and protects its crews from shell splinters and CW/BW agents.*

Performance – gun: Maximum range, unassisted 24,060yd (22,000m); maximum range, rocket-assisted 32,800yd (30,000m); elevation -3 to +75 degrees; traverse 360 degrees.

The M109-series of self-propelled 155mm howitzers have been in service since the early 1960s and provide the core artillery capability for the US Army. The latest version to enter service is the Paladin M109A6, which is the fourth major upgrade and includes significant enhancements in the areas of responsiveness, terminal effects, range and survivability, as well as in reliability and ease-of-maintenance.

The M109A6 is an armored, full-tracked weapon, mounting the M284 howitzer and carrying 37 complete conventional rounds plus two Copperhead projectiles. It has a new, Kevlar-lined turret, which incorporates considerable improvements, as well as a full-width bustle with armor shielding to improve the protection of the propelling charges. The vehicle can travel at a maximum speed of 38mph, and has a cruising range of some 186 miles. When on the move it is normal for the barrel to be held in a travel lock, which used to be secured and released manually, but in the M109A6 is done by remote control.

The Automatic Fire Control System (AFCS) has on-board ballistic computation and automatic weapon pointing, and an integrated inertial navigation system (INS) with embedded GPS processing, which enables a moving M109A6 to receive a fire mission, compute firing data, select and take up a fire position, automatically unlock and point its cannon, and then fire the first round all in under 60 seconds. This "shoot-and-scoot" capability, which is achieved by day or by night, not only significantly improves responsiveness to calls for fire, but also protects the vehicle and crew since they would have left the site before the enemy could respond with counterbattery fire.

The M109A6 uses the M284 cannon assembly which has a new tube, combined with structural improvements to the bore evacuator and muzzle brake, as well as improvements to the breech and recoil system to increase component life. The new M203-series charges provide a maximum range of at least 24,060yd, a dramatic increase over the original M109's maximum range of 16,070yd. Even this excellent range is increased to 32,800yd with rocket assisted projectiles (RAP).

The SPH cannot be considered in isolation from its M992A2 Field Artillery Ammunition Support Vehicle (FAASV); the two comprise a howitzer section and travel together. The FAASV is a tracked vehicle, with the same mobility, survivability and speed as the SPH, and is fitted with a hydraulically powered conveyor for transferring single-rounds to the SPH. The FAASV has a crew of five.

ARTILLERY ROCKET SYSTEMS

Artillery rocket systems produce a heavy concentration of fire at considerable ranges and with great accuracy. Iraq has some elderly Russian and a few modern Yugoslav systems, but the US Army has the Multiple Launch Rocket System (MLRS), which proved a great success in the 1991 Gulf War and has since been improved. The main problem with such systems is their great rate of fire, which imposes a considerable load on the resupply system.

Iraq is even less well armed in rocket systems than in tube artillery. It has a maximum of 50 FROG rocket launchers, mostly FROG-7 mounted on an 8-wheeled ZIL-135 launcher. In the Soviet Army these were nuclear-capable, but the Iraqi rockets are fitted with either HE or chemical warheads. Also in service are a variety of multiple rocket launchers (MRL), including Soviet-supplied 132mm BM-13 and 122mm BM-21, and the Brazilian 127mm ASTROS II. There are also a number of battalions of the Ababeel, a 262mm rocket launcher, which was jointly developed by Iraq and Yugoslavia, but manufactured in Yugoslavia, where it is known as the M-87 *Orkan*.

▲ **Above** *The Frog-7 is a mobile, long-range Soviet system, but Iraq has only some 50 launchers. Rockets can carry HE or chemical warheads.*

Caliber	Weapon	Origin	Range (miles)	Rounds per launcher	Warhead (HE)
122mm	BM-21	USSR	9.4	40	HE – 14.5lb
127mm	ASTROS 2*	Brazil	8.7	12	HE – 77.2lb
128mm	M-77 *Organj*	Yugoslavia	12.5	32	HE – 11lb
132mm	BM-13	USSR	5.6	16	HE/chemical
262mm	M-87 *Orkan***	Yugoslavia	31.2	12	HE/chemical
600mm	Frog-7	USSR	40.6	1	HE/chemical

* Sajil   ** Ababeel-50   **Iraqi artillery rocket systems**

This is mounted on an 8 x 8 heavy truck chassis. There is also another Yugoslav-supplied system, the *M-77 Organj*, which mounts 32 128mm rockets on a 6 x 6 truck.

The major significance of the larger rocket systems is that the Iraqis have developed chemical warheads for them, many of which – but almost certainly not all – were destroyed by the UN teams following the 1991 Gulf War. This will inevitably make them priority targets for US counterbattery fire missions and air strikes. On the US side the equipment is one system only, the excellent and well-proven MLRS.

▶ **Right** *Iraq uses the aged, Soviet-supplied BM-21 122mm rocket system*

Multiple Launch Rocket System (MLRS)

Manufacturer: Lockheed Martin Vought, USA.

Type: Carrier/launcher for MLRS system.

Crew: 3 (driver, gunner, section chief).

Rocket: 600lb (272kg); length 13ft (4.0m), diameter 8.9in (227mm); speed >Mach 1.0; range >18.6 miles (30km); warhead 644 x M42 bomblets.

Dimensions: Length 271in (7.0m); width 116in (3.0m); height 102in (2.6m).

Weight: 61,600lb (28.,000kg).

Engine: Cummins, VTA-903T, Vee-8; turbo-charged; 506bhp at 2.600rpm.

Performance - vehicle: Maximum speed 40mph (64km/h); range 302 miles (483km); gradient 60 percent; step 3.3ft (1m); fording depth (without preparation) 43in (1.1m).

▲ **Above** *The US Army MLRS is a very powerful weapon; Iraqis quickly learnt to dread its rockets in the 1991 war and will do so again in 2003.*

Continued over

▲ **Above** *A US artilleryman feeds data into the computer controlling the operation of his MLRS system, which can launch up to 12 rockets in less than one minute; effect on the target is devastating in power and accuracy.*

The Multiple Launch Rocket System (MLRS) entered service with the US Army in 1983, its primary mission being to suppress, neutralize or destroy hostile fire support, mechanized units, armored formations and air defense targets. Without leaving their cab, the crew can launch 12 rockets (2 pods) within one minute, which will devastate an area target covering some 550 x 550yd at a maximum range of 49,200yd. MLRS is designed to get into and out of action and reload quickly, enabling it to attack time-urgent targets and also to avoid enemy counterbattery fire. Significant numbers of MLRS launchers were fielded by both the US and British armies in Operation Desert Storm and performed very well. Following this combat experience, improvement programs were set in hand to enhance its already formidable capabilities, including greater range, improved fire control system and improved launcher mechanical systems.

The warhead of the M26 rocket contains 644 M77 dual-purpose submunitions, each of which detonates on impact; they can penetrate up to 4in armor or produce an anti-personnel effect with a lethal radius of some 13ft. One of the major problems with a high rate of fire rocket system is that of resupply and MLRS is no exception. Each battery of nine launchers has its own ammunition platoon of 18 resupply vehicles and trailers, and there are more further back in the logistic system.

The upgraded MLRS M270A1 was fielded in September 2000 and includes the Improved Fire Control System (IFCS), the Improved Mechanical Launch System (IMLS), and the extended range rocket (ER-MLRS). The IFCS is designed to avoid the problem of electronic obsolescence and also includes measures to accommodate new missiles. The ILES speeds up response times, by reducing aiming time from 93 seconds to 16 seconds, and cutting reload time by some 38 percent and reload times by 50 percent. The improvements combine to reduce the time in the launch site by 60 percent and to increase system reliability by 45 percent.

INFANTRY WEAPONS

There is a wide range of weaponry available to the infantry of both the US and Iraqi forces, including rifles, grenades, machine guns, mortars, and shoulder- and vehicle-launched missiles for anti-tank and air defense missions. The US Army infantryman and Marine are better equipped and more effectively armed now than ever in the nation's history. His 5.56mm M16A2 semi-automatic rifle is a very reliable and effective weapon, light and easy to carry. Each squad also carries at least one M249 Squad Automatic Weapon (SAW).

Other weapons available include sniper rifles of various types including the increasingly popular Barrett 0.50in "Light Fifty" anti-materiel rifle, 0.50in M2HB machine gun, and a plethora of weapons under company and battalion control, as well as those mounted on the IFVs and APCs. All these combine to give a modern US infantry battalion devastating resources of firepower, coupled to a high degree of mobility.

On the other side of the hill the Iraqi infantryman is armed with predominantly Russian-designed weaponry, including the 7.62mm AK-47 and 5.56mm AK-74 rifles, 7.62mm RPK machine gun, SVD sniper rifle, and a variety of ground- and vehicle-launched anti-tank guided missiles (ATGM). At least some of this equipment and ammunition is now manufactured in Iraq, but is very unlikely to match US equipment, in either technology or sophistication.

One area in which the Iraqi infantry is well provided for is in mortars. These weapons are known in most armies as the "battalion commander's artillery" since they are the major fire support asset under his

▼ **Below** *Marines of a Force Recon unit, armed with M16A2 rifles. This rifle has served US troops well for some 40 years and is an excellent weapon, combining hitting power and good range with reliability*

◀ **Left** *The US Barrett M82 "Light 50" is a very powerful 0.5 caliber sniping rifle.*

▲ **Above** *RPK 7.62mm machine gun, one of many infantry weapons supplied to Iraq by the USSR. These weapons are rugged and reliable, but their effective use also depends upon the determination of the man firing them.*

▼ **Below** *This Soviet-supplied M-1952 240mm heavy mortar is large, difficult to conceal, and lacks any protection for the Iraqi crew.*

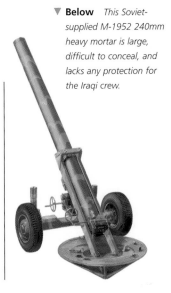

direct command. Mortars are capable of rapid, high-angle, plunging fire. This is invaluable against dug-in enemy troops and targets behind cover, which cannot be effectively engaged by direct fire from other weapons in an infantry battalion. Thus, mortars provide a very effective means of bringing heavy fire to bear both speedily and accurately, while their light weight and simplicity of operation make them ideal for bringing into and out of action quickly, and moving rapidly from one fire position to another.

The US Army has three calibers of mortar currently in service: 60mm, 81mmm and 120mm. The Iraqi Army not only has light 51mm mortars, and 81mm and 120mm, of similar performance to US models, except for shorter ranges, but also has two much heavier types: 160mm and 240mm caliber. There are also reports that Iraq is manufacturing its own mortars and ammunition, and that some 160mm mortars have been mounted on surplus tank chassis.

Type	US Mortars		Iraqi Mortars		
	M224	M252	M120	M-1953	M-240
Bore	60mm	81mm	120mm	160mm	240mm
Length, barrel	40in (102cm)	56in (142cm)	69in (175cm)	14.5ft (4.5m)	17.7ft (5.4m)
Weight, combat	46.5lb (21.1kg)	89lb (40.4kg)	319lb (145kg)	2,870lb (1,300kg)	7,960lb (3,610kg)
Weight, 1 round HE	4lb (1.8kg)	15lb (6.8kg)	33lb (15kg)	91lb (41.5kg)	220lb (100kg)
Max range	3,817yd (3,490m)	6,234yd (5,700m)	7,874yd (7,200m)	9,200yd (8,400m)	10,600yd (9,700m)
Rates of fire sustained	20rpm	8rpm	4 rpm	3rpm	<1rpm
Crew	2	3	5	7	8

US and Iraqi mortars

▲ **Above** *US Marines with M224 60mm mortars. These weapons provide rapid and very effective fire at platoon and company level in infantry and Marine units; they are particularly valued for their quick response.*

▲ **Above** *Ground-launched air defense missiles are an increasing danger to low-flying aircraft; these 160th Special Ops Squadron AC-130Hs are firing decoy flares to protect themselves as they come in to deliver SOF to a landing zone.*

▲ **Above** *Unlike Desert Storm, the 2003 war will involve US forces fighting in the cities. This has always been a costly and difficult operation, but US soldiers, including these Marines, have been undergoing special training with new equipment*

US SPECIAL OPERATIONS FORCES

In the 1991 Gulf War, the Coalition's Special Operations Forces (SOF) played a most significant role in ground operations, with US, British and French SOF operating deep inside Iraqi territory. They had various missions, the highest profile being the location, and in some cases, the destruction of Iraqi Scud launcher sites. In a future conflict, US SOF will be fighting their own battles deep inside Iraqi territory. Some of their operations will be in support of operations by conventional troops, some will be strategic military missions, such as once again hunting Scud launch sites, and some will be other, even more clandestine "unconventional" tasks, possibly even against the very highest levels of the Iraqi leadership. The US SOF personnel will be found from a number of units.

1st Special Forces Operational Detachment – Delta

1st Special Forces Operational Detachment – Delta (1SFOD-Delta), more familiarly known as just "Delta," is based at Fort Bragg. It is composed of a headquarters and

◀ **Left** *"Delta" soldiers were among the Special Ops forces that carried out hazardous Scud-hunting missions during the 1991 Gulf War. Here, General Schwarzkopf thanks them after Desert Storm.*

▼ **Below** *US Army Rangers fast-rope into a landing zone from a 160th Special Operations Aviation Regiment (SOAR) MH-47 Chinook.*

three operational squadrons, each of which is composed of two or more troops, each of four 4-man squads. There are also a support squadron, a communications squadron, and a covert troop using special equipment and techniques. The main aviation support for Delta comes from 160th Special Operations Aviation Regiment (160SOAR) but Delta also has its own aviation troop which uses helicopters with civilian color schemes and registration. Delta has carried out many special operations. During Operation Desert Storm it deployed to Iraq to work alongside British, Australian, and New Zealand SAS units in seeking out and destroying Scud missile launchers.

US Army Rangers (Airborne)

Today there are approximately 2,500 Rangers in the 75th Ranger Regiment, whose headquarters and 3rd Battalion (3/75) are at Fort Benning, Georgia, with 1/75 at Hunter Army Field, Georgia, and 2/75 at Fort Lewis, Washington. Each of these three battalions has a headquarters and three combat companies, each with three rifle platoons and a weapons platoon.

▼ **Below** *US Navy SEALs prepare inflatable dinghies and other equipment, prior to leaving a surfaced nuclear submarine. Some SEAL units have participated in extraction of specific individuals.*

All troops are volunteers from elsewhere in the Army and have passed the Ranger course. They remain with the Rangers for a standard two-year tour, which can be extended by six months, subject to recommendation by the commanding officer. 75th Ranger Regiment is an Army unit, but operationally it comes under the Joint Special Operations Command (JSOC) and each of the three battalions takes it in turn to be the "Ranger Ready Force" for a month at a time, which requires it to be ready to deploy anywhere in the world within 18 hours. On deployment, the Ranger units can be required to operate on their own or as part of a larger force made up of different units, as, for example, on the ill-fated Teheran Embassy rescue mission (Operation Eagle Claw, 1979).

Sea, Air Land (SEAL) Teams

Apart from the one water exit through the Shatt el-Arab into the Gulf, Iraq is an essentially landlocked country and it is unlikely (although by no means impossible) that there will be great requirement for the usual naval and underwater skills of the SEAL teams. However, SEAL Team Three which covers the Middle East is likely to be involved, as is SEAL Team 6 which has been involved in operations targeted at extracting specific individuals – for example, alleged war criminals in the former Yugoslavia – and it may do the same in Iraq.

▲ **Above** *US SOF infiltrate in many ways but one of the most spectacular is sitting on the outside of the MH-6J "Little Bird," a very small but highly capable helicopter which has given valuable service for many years.*

MH-60 Blackhawk

Manufacturer: Sikorsky, USA.

Type: Special Operations Forces helicopter.

Weight: Maximum takeoff with external load 23,500lb (10,660kg).

Dimensions: Length, rotors turning, 64.8ft (19.8m); width, fuselage 7.8ft (2.4m); rotor diameter 53.8ft (16.4m); height 16.9ft (5.2m).

Powerplant: Two GE T700-GE-701C turboshafts, each 1,870shp max.

Performance: Maximum speed 195kt (225mph/362km/h); service ceiling 19,150ft (5,840m); self-deployment range 1,150nm (1,330 miles/2,140km).

Armament: Two 6-barrel 7.62mm miniguns (DAP – see notes).

Crew: 2 flight crew plus up to 14 fully equipped passengers.

Continued over

▲ **Above**   *The main helicopter used by US Army Special Operations Forces is the MH-60 Blackhawk, which is fitted for aerial refueling (probe is below cockpit), thus enabling it to operate deep inside enemy territory.*

The 160th SOAR(A) operates three models of the MH-60 Blackhawk: MH-60K, MH-60L and MH-60L(DAP). The primary mission of the MH-60 is to conduct infiltration, exfiltration, and resupply of SOF across a wide range of environmental conditions, while secondary missions include carrying external loads, CSAR and MEDEVAC operations. An armed version, the Direct Action Penetrator (DAP), has the primary mission of armed escort and fire support.

The MH-60K is a highly modified version of the Army's standard twin engine utility helicopter, the modifications including aerial refueling capability, advanced aircraft survivability equipment, and improved navigation systems; 23 have been delivered to Army SOF. The MH-60L is a modified version of the standard US Army UH-60L, configured for special operations use with an updated cockpit, additional avionics, precision navigation system, FLIR, aircraft survivability equipment, and an external tank system.

The MH-60L Direct Action Penetrator (DAP) is an MH-60L which has been further modified to mount a variety of offensive weapons systems to enable it to conduct attack helicopter operations during day, night, or adverse weather conditions. It can provide armed escort for employment against threats to a helicopter formation. Using team tactics, the DAP is capable of providing suppression or close air support (CAS) for formations and teams on the ground. The MH-60 DAP has integrated fire control systems and a pilot's head-up display (HUD). The DAP is capable of mounting two M-134 7.62mm miniguns, two 30mm chain guns, two 19-round 2.75in (70mm) rocket pods, and Hellfire and Stinger missiles in a variety of combinations. The 7.62 miniguns remain with the aircraft regardless of the mission.

▲ **Above** *Air gunner with his Minigun in the cabin of an MH-60 SOF helicopter. It is vital for such aircraft to be able to suppress enemy fire as they come in to infiltrate or exfiltrate ground troops.*

MH-47D/E Chinook

Manufacturer: Boeing, USA.

Type: Special Operations Forces medium-lift helicopter.

Weight: Maximum take-off 54,000lb (24,490kg).

Dimensions: length, rotors turning, 99ft (30m); width, blades folded, 12.4ft (3.8m); maximum height 18.9ft (5.76m).

Powerplant: Two AlliedSignal T55-L741s turboshafts, each 4,867shp max.

Performance: Maximum speed 145knots (168mph/270km/h); service ceiling 10,150ft (3,094m); self-deployment range 1,260nm (1,456miles/2,342km).

Armament: 2-4 machine guns (see notes).

Payload: 33 to 55 troops or 24 litters and 2 attendants.

Crew: 2 pilots plus provision for combat commander.

The MH-47 is a twin-engined, tandem rotor, heavy assault helicopter based on the CH-47 airframe, and conducts overt and covert infiltrations, exfiltrations, air assault, resupply, and sling operations over a wide range of environmental conditions. With the use of special mission equipment and night vision devices, the air crew can operate in hostile mission environments over all types of terrain at low altitudes during periods of low visibility and low ambient lighting conditions with pinpoint navigation accuracy of plus/minus 30 seconds on target. MH-47s can be transported in C-5 and C-17 transport aircraft (two in each), or can self-deploy over extended distances using ground or aerial refueling.

There are two current models: MH-47D Adverse Weather Cockpit (AWC) – operated by 3/160, and the MH-47E – operated by 2/160. The MH-47D (AWC) is equipped with weather avoidance/search radar; an aerial refueling probe for in-flight refueling; a personnel locator system (PLS) used in conjunction with the PRC-112 radio for finding downed aircrews, FLIR, and other special-to-role equipment. It carries a defensive armament system consisting of two M-134 machine guns (left forward cabin window, right cabin door) and one M-60D machine gun located on the ramp, and an internal rescue hoist with a 600lb capacity. The MH-47E has other specialized equipment; 25 are currently operated and planned upgrades include aircraft systems modifications, avionics system upgrades, and aircraft survivability enhancements.

▲ **Above** *The many versions of the Chinook have served since the Vietnam War; this is an MH-47 SOF version, recognizable by its massive refueling probe, enabling it to self-deploy over great distances*

Desert Patrol/Light Strike Vehicle

Manufacturer: Chenowyth Racing, USA.

Type: Desert patrol vehicle.

Crew: 3.

Armament: See notes.

Armor: None.

Dimensions: length 13.4ft (4.1m); height 6.6ft (2.0m); width 7.9ft (2.4m).

Weight: gross vehicle weight 2,700lb (1,225kg).

Engine: Volkswagen gasoline engine; 200hp.

Performance: Maximum road speed <60mph (97km/h); acceleration 0-30mph (0-49km/h) in 4sec; range <200 miles (322km); maximum slope 75 percent; maximum side slope 50 percent; ground clearance 16in (41cm); payload 1,500lb (680kg).

One of the few vehicles developed specifically for SOF, the Desert Patrol Vehicle (DPV) is a joint program between the Marine Corps and Special Operations Command (USSOCOM). It is a modified version of the off-road, three-man, 2 x 4 racing vehicle built by Chenowyth Racing of El Cajon, California. It is designed to provide greater mobility than the HMMWV ("Hummer") and operate anywhere a four-wheel drive vehicle can, but with greater speed and increased maneuverability. The DPV is air-transportable in most fixed-wing transport aircraft; the C-130, for example, can carry four, the CH-53 Super Stallion and the MH-47D Chinook two each.

This high performance vehicle can perform numerous combat roles including: special operations delivery, rescue of downed aircrew, command and control, weapons platform, rear area combat operations, reconnaissance, forward observation/lasing team, military police, artillery forward observer transport, etc. The vehicle has three weapons stations, which can accommodate any three from: Mk19 40mm automatic grenade launcher, 0.50in (12.7mm) M2HB machine gun, M60 7.62 machine gun, AT-4 anti-tank missile, low-recoil 30mm cannon, and TOW missile launcher. Hand-held missile launchers such as Dragon and Stinger can also be carried.

The vehicle is currently operated only by SEAL Team Three, which covers the Middle East theater of operations and normally deploys them in pairs for mutual support. It will in future be operated more widely, the new vehicles being due to enter service in 2004-05, although some will undoubtedly have been rushed into production in anticipation of the war with Iraq.

▲ **Above** *The three-man Desert Patrol Vehicle is very small, has a high performance, and was developed specially for desert conditions to enable SOF to move rapidly and with minimum visual or acoustic signatures.*

160th Special Operations Aviation Regiment (Airborne)

160SOAR is assigned to the US Army Special Operations Command (SOCOM) and its aircraft have taken part in many US actions including those in Grenada, Panama, the Persian Gulf, and Somalia. The regiment comprises three aviation battalions, with 1/160 and 2/160 at Fort Campbell, Kentucky, and 3/160 at Hunter Army Airfield, Georgia. Special operations helicopters are also operated by 1st Battalion, 245th Aviation Regiment of the Oklahoma Army National Guard. The main helicopters in use by 160SOAR are various versions of the MH-60 and MH-47, but there are also numbers of the much smaller MH-6.

IRAQI SPECIAL OPERATIONS FORCES

As described above, the Iraqi Special Forces Brigades do not (so far as is known) have a role equivalent to Western SOF. However, there is another force, under the control of the Security Directorate, that does.

Brigade 999

Iraqi military intelligence operates a brigade-size formation of six 300-men battalions, whose missions and activities are similar to those of the Russian *Spetsnaz* troops, which caused such alarm in NATO countries during the Cold War. Designated Brigade 999, the Iraqi unit has its headquarters at Salman Pak (where the *Fedayeen Saddam* also conducts training courses) and its known operations have included sabotage of Iranian oil facilities, as well as infiltration and disruption of dissident military units in Kurdistan. The brigade is also believed to have made a plan to kidnap or kill General Schwarzkopf during Desert Storm. As with the *Spetsnaz*, each battalion specializes in a particular mission and geographical area as indicated by its unit title:

- **1st (Persian) Battalion.** Targets in Iran.
- **2nd (Saudi Arabia) Battalion.** Targets in Saudi Arabia and Gulf states.
- **3rd (Palestine) Battalion.** Targets in Israel.
- **4th (Turkish) Battalion.** Targets in the north including Turkey and Kurdistan.
- **5th (Marine) Battalion.** Operations at sea including naval mine warfare.
- **6th (Opposition) Battalion.** Operations against Iraqi dissidents, both at home and abroad.

In the event of an attack by the US, men of Brigade 999 could deploy to other Middle Eastern countries to conduct or to inspire operations by the local population against the United States and its allies. Such operations might include sabotage attacks on ports, airfields, roads and railways, depots, barracks, transit camps and other "soft targets." The brigade might also plan to operate inside the homelands of the USA and its wartime partners in order to disrupt the mobilization of resources and to encourage anti-war movements. No details are known of special aircraft or equipment operated by Brigade 999.

▲ **Above** *Men of 75th Ranger Regiment training for Military Operations in Urban Terrain (MOUT), in anticipation of fighting in Iraqi cities.*

> ❝Iraq's Brigade 999 is believed to have made a plan to kidnap or kill General Schwarzkopf during Desert Storm.❞

AMERICA'S ALLIES

"The time for denying, deceiving, and delaying has come to an end. Saddam Hussein must disarm himself – or, for the sake of peace, we will lead a coalition to disarm him. Many nations are joining us in insisting that Saddam Hussein's regime be held accountable. They are committed to defending the international security that protects the lives of both our citizens and theirs."
– President George W. Bush, 2 October, 2002

America's search for allies will continue right up to the day before the invasion starts, but by the end of 2002 only a very few nations had shown any willingness to give serious consideration to participation, let alone make any firm promises to join forces with the United States.

United Kingdom

The only major country to have made a firm and unequivocal commitment to take part is the UK, which will provide some 20-25,000 soldiers, sailors and airmen. The actual forces likely to be involved are some or all of the following:

- 1st (UK) Armoured Division, consisting of two armored brigades, plus the normal divisonal units, such as artillery, engineers, aviation., communications, and logistic troops, but also probably reinforced with additional artillery, engineer and aviation elements.
- A number of RAF squadrons equipped with Panavia Tornado strike, reconnaissance and fighter aircraft, and also one or more squadrons of Jaguar ground attack aircraft.
- RAF detachments, including aerial tankers and transport aircraft
- RN carrier battle group in the Gulf, plus Tomahawk-armed SSN submarines in the Red Sea.
- Special forces, including Special Air Service and Special Boat Service.
- A national support command, providing UK command, administrative and logistic support to the UK combat elements.

▲ **Above** *British infantry have a long tradition of desert operations, and also share common operating procedures, language and traditions with US forces. Note the fixed bayonets, still a favorite weapon with British troops!*

All UK combat elements will serve under US command. However, as is usual in such circumstances, there will be a separate national command and administrative element, which will report back direct to the UK government in London.

Two major items of equipment which will form part of the UK force will be the Challenger 2 main battle tank and Tornado strike aircraft:

Challenger 2 Main Battle Tank

Country of origin: UK.

Crew: 4

Armament: One Royal Ordnance L30A1 120mm rifled gun; one Hughes L94A1 7.62mm chain gun coaxial with the main gun; one L37A2 7.62mm remote-controlled machine gun on turret roof.

Armor: Second generation, Chobham type.

Dimensions: Length 37ft 8in (11.5m); width 11ft 6in (3.52m); height (to turret roof) 8ft 2in (2.5m).

▲ **Above** *The main difference between this British Challenger 2 and the US M1 is that it has a rifled 120mm main gun, enabling it to fire HESH/HEP rounds.*

Weight: Combat 137,500lb (62,500kg).

Ground pressure: 12.8lb/sq in (0.9kg/sq cm).

Engine: Perkins CV-12 TA Condor V-12 12-cylinder diesel; 1,200bhp at 2,300rpm.

Performance: Road speed 35mph (56km/h); range 280 miles (450km); vertical obstacle 2ft 10in (0.9m); trench 7ft 8in (2.34m); gradient 60 percent

There will be at least four armored regiments with 1(UK) Armoured Division, equipped with the British Challenger 2 tank. The British Army took delivery in the late 1990s of 269 Challenger 2 MBTs. They are armed with the new Royal Ordnance L30 rifled gun, which is fitted, as is normal practice, with a thermal sleeve, fume extractor and muzzle reference system. Sixty-four projectiles are carried, together with 42 charges, the latter being stowed in armored boxes below the turret ring for maximum safety.

It is noteworthy that the Challenger 2 was the only new MBT in the 1990s to mount a rifled main gun, as opposed to smoothbore 120mm guns, as mounted in the US Army's M1A2, for example. The reason for this is the British Army's continuing belief, reinforced by its experiences in the Gulf War in 1991, in the value of the HESH round (known as HEP in the US Army). When such a round hits a tank the high-explosive forms, for the briefest moment, a circular "cake" which is then exploded by a charge in the base of the projectile. The shock from this explosion dislodges a large scab from the inside wall of the tank, and this then ricochets at high velocity around the crew compartment.

▲ **Above** *Britain's Tornado F3 fighter, has been deployed in the Gulf for many years. It is similar to the Tornado GR.4, but is optimized for air combat missions and is armed with air-to-air missiles.*

Tornado

Manufacturer: Panavia, UK/Germany/Italy.

Type: Multi-role strike/ground attack aircraft.

Weight: Empty 30,620lb (13,890kg); max takeoff 61,620lb (27,950kg).

Dimensions: Length 54ft 10in (16.7m); height 19ft 6in (5.95m); wingspan (25 degree sweep) 28ft 3in (8.6m).

Powerplant: Two Turbo-Union RB199-34R Mk 103 turbofans, each 9,100lb (40kN) dry and 16,075lb (70kN) with afterburner.

Performance: Max level speed (clean) Mach 1.3; with external stores Mach 0.92; combat radius (hi-lo-hi) 750nm (1,390km); ferry range 2,100nm (3,890km).

Armament: One IWKA Mauser 27mm cannon; 19,840lb (9,000kg) on three underfuselage and four underwing hardpoints, including AIM-9s, iron bombs, laser guided bombs, ALARM and HARM anti-radiation missiles, JP233 and MW-1 area denial weapon dispensers.

Crew: Two.

(Data are for Tornado GR.4.)

◀ **Left** *The Royal Air Force Tornado GR.4 is a very capable strike platform used in Desert Storm and in the many attacks on Iraq since 1991 which have been intended to compel Saddam to comply with UN resolutions.*

The RAF operates three versions of the Panavia Tornado: GR4 strike, GR.4A reconnaissance and F.3 air defense fighter, although there are some of the unconverted GR.1s still in service. The GR.4 is a rebuilt GR.1 with Forward Looking InfraRed (FLIR), GPS, improved avionics, an NVG (Night Vision Goggles) compatible cockpit, and greater compatibility with precision guided weapons, such as Paveway III laser-guided bombs, Brimstone anti-tank guided missiles and Storm Shadow anti-ship missiles.

The GR.4A is a parallel upgrade to the GR.1A reconnaissance version. Unlike the GR.1, the GR.4 and GR.4A do not have cannon mounted in the forward fuselage, the space being needed for the Sideways Looking Infra-Red system and a Linescan infra-red surveillance system, which require a small window in the side of the fuselage, just below the cockpit.

During the 1991 Gulf War, Tornados suffered the highest casualties of Allied aircraft, largely due to them being employed against heavily defended airfields. Early on they had to fly at heights of a few hundred feet, dictated by requirements of the JP233 airfield-attack munition. Within three days, however, Iraqi combat air operations had almost ceased, allowing the Tornado crews to switch weapons to LGBs and conventional 1,000lb bombs, and to move to higher altitude.

Gulf States

The Gulf States owe the United States an unquantifiable debt for leading the Coalition that kicked Saddam Hussein's forces out of Kuwait in 1991. It is thus probable that they will provide basing facilities and airfields, as well as some combat aircraft, and may also form a composite brigade to take part in the land battle.

Israel

One country that is very likely to be involved in the 2003 war is Israel, even though its participation will be very controversial with the Arab allies of the United States. Israel was targeted by Saddam's Scud missiles during the 1991 war in an effort to force it to join the hostilities (and thereby weaken the willingness of the Coalition's Arab forces to be involved), but the US administration persuaded Israel to stay out. Despite denials at the time, it later became known that Sayeret Mak'tal, one of Israel's most proficient special forces units, had deployed to Iraq to find Scud launch sites, although with what success is not known. In November 2002 it was reliably reported that Mat'kal patrols were once again in Iraq, involved in reconnoitering potential Scud launch sites, to enable even more rapid responses next time around.

Australia

Australia is known to be keen to take part. Forces committed may include special forces (Australian Special Air Service), a small ground contingent, and aircraft.

▼ **Below** *Men of Israel's Mak'tal, an elite SOF unit. They may deploy in a future war with Iraq, but this would be very unpopular with Arab countries.*

INDEX

Figures in **bold** type indicate references in captions to illustrations.